TIME TO
REALLY
LIVE FREE

DARLENE GASTON

ISBN 978-1-0980-1428-5 (paperback)
ISBN 978-1-0980-1429-2 (digital)

Christian Faith Publishing, Inc.
832 Park Avenue
Meadville, PA 16335
www.christianfaithpublishing.com

Printed in the United States of America

I dedicate this book to those who came before me, those who walked with me and for those who come after me. You all know who you are and I am grateful for each one of you. You are the church walking out the truth in every day life.

CONTENTS

RELIGIOUS?!?

Have you ever said, "No, I am not religious… I have a relationship with God!" I have so many times. I was explaining to my family, the other day, how I had truly felt like I had a relationship with God before my revelation. I prayed for one to three hours daily. I watched my words. I wanted to prove to God and others I loved him with all my heart, soul, mind, and body; I wanted my boys to choose God's free gift, live a "favored life," and be obedient little soldiers of Christ through a "relationship with him." I needed to prove to God I wanted to live a holy life for him. God and I did have "relationship," but it wasn't exactly the way he wanted it. It was much more religious than it was a relationship, and I had chosen to make it that way because this is what I had learned to do in the church. Church leaders had taught me you choose God's free gift then you work to keep the free gift.

Church leaders had taught me you choose God's free gift then you work to keep the free gift.

It might help to first define the word *religious*. This is a difficult word to define as it uses the word in the definition. The definition according to Merriam-Webster is:

> member of a religious order, congregation, etc.; a monk, friar, or nun. the religious, devout or religious persons. devoted, unswerving, meticulous.

I was definitely devoted, unswerving, and meticulous. I am not saying these are bad things to be. Just like with many things, they can have both a positive or negative effect. My devotion, steadfastness, and diligence to my checklist of things I must do to keep God happy actually usurped God himself.

My devotion, steadfastness, and diligence to my checklist of things I must do to keep God happy actually usurped God himself.

This is how I define religious: when your checklist usurps God himself. You may think you are not religious and maybe you aren't. I was religious and thought I was just really "loving God." But loving God should not feel like a requirement to receive his love. This is where I found myself living from. It is easy for me to see now, but back then, I couldn't see the heavy burden I was carrying around by trying to make God happy with me by proving I love him. I think when you hear what he has to say about the way he views relationship and take a look at some examples of core beliefs you may hold, then you will also have your own personal revelation. From this revelation, I am believing you will, like me, have a shift in your core beliefs. If you are tired of performing for God's love and acceptance, if you have found the yoke is heavy instead of light, then I invite you on this adventure with me, which will lead into a wide open space you could only have imagine before. It is a place, which is fuller of rest, love, grace, and mercy. It is simple and the message has always been there. I believe this book brings us full circle back to the original teaching Jesus brought to earth and his disciples passed on. It is the message, which has been lost in many mainstream churches, but there are always voices proclaiming the truth through the generations. Come and live free with me, the way Jesus intended. For whom the son sets free is free indeed. This is my prayer for each of us as we go on this adventure together.

CHRISTIAN CAREER

I wasn't always religious. Actually, I talked to God all the time when I was a little girl. He and I were having conversations all of the time when I needed to talk or ask him to help me find something or just be with him. He was always there for me, and it was simple. There was no need to wonder, "Is this God's voice?" I just knew it was. A simple childlike faith. These times with him were so comforting for me. When I was in junior high school, I had asked him to do something for me. I wanted him to keep my best friend from moving away. This was the first time I felt he did not do what I had asked for. Anyone ever feel like that? My friend and her family moved far away. I didn't understand, at this time, that people have a free will and God couldn't force my opinion on my friend's family. As many teenagers do, I got mad at him for not doing what I wanted him to. For the most part, I stopped talking to him and went out on my own. So many choices made between those years and my midtwenties. I found out life without talking to him was pretty miserable. Did I figure that out quickly? No. I had so many bad choices piled up in the later half of my twenties: sex outside of marriage, drinking to be intoxicated, abortions, and lying. I pretty much hated the choices I had made, which led to hating myself for making those choices. Looking back now, I was a mess. Thankfully, God *always* has a plan for every single person, and he had one for me. I met a man, Bryan, who would later become my husband, and he reintroduced God into my life. Not in a religious way, but in a way that reminded me God was for me, loved me, and desired to have a relationship with me. At the age of twenty-seven, I decided to go to a "tent meeting" at Bryan's church where I accepted Jesus's free gift. At the end of the sermon, it was customary to ask if anyone had accepted Jesus into their heart; and if you had, they requested you to raise your hand so they could talk to you. I raised my hand and was asked to go back to talk with someone to make sure I understood the choice I had just made. To help me understand my choice, scriptures were read to me, and I was asked if I agreed with what was read. One of those scriptures stood out to me because of four words. The scripture was from 1 John 1:17, "But if we walk in the Light as He Himself is in the Light, we have fellowship with one another, and the blood of Jesus His Son *cleanses us from all sin*" (NASB; emphasis mine). The five words, "cleanses us from all sin," changed me in that moment. I walked out of the back of the church feeling as white as the driven snow. All my wrongs have been cleared, God loves me, and all is right in my world. I felt so good and wonderful for a few weeks. I got baptized, and a few days later, life happens and I mess up. I sinned again as a *believer* and my question became, "What do I now do with this new sin I have committed as a Christian?" In the church, through scripture, I learned how to repent and ask/beg God to forgive my inadequacies in not holding up my end of the bargain ("sinning"). As time went on, I began to also "learn in the church" just how my behavior would dictate whether or not I stayed in favor with God or maybe even "maintained my salvation" with God. What I was learning at church became more and more difficult for me to perform. My behavior wasn't perfect enough, according to the church teaching, to keep God happy with me. I was learning; if I didn't perform well enough to keep him happy, then I should expect him to turn away from me and give me a good spanking. The spanking would be in the form of no favor from him, curses, demonic warfare, sickness, and ruin for myself and/or my family. I lived in a constant state of fear, trying to make things right with God again and again.

I didn't understand, at the time, how our own human-ness desires to make things "right with God." I, like every-one else I saw in the church, just wanted to perform well for God. It was expected; it was what I experienced in the church. Behavior was closely looked at... I mean WWJD (What would Jesus do?) I was told: think about what he would do and do that! As I sat, watched, and listened, I learned: behave well so Jesus will not earn more strips on my behalf; if you really love him, then you will behave properly and you will be obedient to him in everything; if you want to be considered a "good Christian," you had better prove you have all the right qualities a good Christian should have; if you want to climb up the corporate—ooops, the church ladder—you need to attain a certain level of holiness for God to use you; if you want to be "used by God," you need to make sure you stay pure or clean enough for God; if you want favor with God, your behavior better line up with God's liking or else no favor; and many more beliefs (we will call these core beliefs) that were taught to me, using both scripture and behavior, within the church.

Ten years into my "salvation," I had a handful of prophetic words calling out "my ministry." I understood it would be in his timing, but please remember: I believed I had to perform for God and "church leadership" to hold up my part of God's plan. If I didn't hold up my part of the bargain, God's plan would never materialize in my life.

Ten more years and I am at what both I and "the church" would consider the pinnacle of my "Christian career." I have climbed the church ladder, performing my best for God and church leadership. I have been publicly called out at the church I attended as the prophet of the church. I am not only recognized as a prophet by the lead pastors, but also by the people in the congregation. I have made it to my "ultimate Christian goal." I am going to be used by God, walking in what he had planned for me. I am excited to get the prophetic ministry rolling in my church and see people's lives impacted by God. Then everything changed one morning with one sentence I heard from God. My life turned upside down, or maybe it finally turned right side up. One day I woke up and God said to me, "It is time to let go of the rules, Darlene." This was the beginning of my "three days with God." A huge revelation for me and my family in which I gained personal understanding of just who God is and who I am in him.

With this revelation, I ended up losing everything that I had thought, at one time, was important. My "Christian career" ended for many reasons. One of those reasons is because I had been called out as a prophet, I had to be discredited. Otherwise, what I was saying might spread and infect others in the church. Lies were told about me just like the Pharisees and Sadducees did with Jesus. It was painful, yet remarkable, to live through this time and experience a little of what Jesus did at the hands of the religious teachers and elite. I had written this public post, which is true:

Darlene Gaston
Monday at 10:19 AM · ⚖

Church leaders (yes I have been one of those) for far too long have tried to control His sheep by setting rules, regulations and standards in order to "protect" them BUT what it actually does is puts them in bondage (back under the law). God is desiring to tear down this core value because it is based on FEAR not FAITH.

👍 Like   💬 Comment   ➤ Share

So many people were liking the statement I had made above, except the religious leadership of the church my family and I attended. I could not and would not go back to the old way of believing for anyone or anything. My family could not either. We were told to leave our church we had attended for the last nine-plus years (which is a story for another book). We had all been changed from the inside out by God himself, and now it is time to share what I learned with you.

THE PERFECT STORM

Prior to God telling me to "let go of the rules," there were several things that lined up for the "perfect storm." I believe God's timing is perfect, and through everything in my life, he was bringing me to this point where I could understand what real relationship with him is and be able to convey to others what he showed me. Our ability to understand what God is saying to us is filtered through our core beliefs. In the past, I believed my good performance was needed to stay in relationship with God. God wanted to change my core beliefs to line up with his truth, so he and I could actually be in the relationship his son had died for. So to say that three days literally changed my life is true… Yet I know now, God was trying to help me all along, and he wants to help all of us live from a place of truth, rest, life, and love. God is talking to us all the time, saying exactly what we need in each moment of our lives. When I look back now, I can see how God was answering my prayer to help me see him like he sees me (1 Corinthians 13:12).

The perfect storm began when I had gone to a prophetic conference. One of the speakers was talking about core values, and I asked the Lord, "I want to know my core values." God decided to do something better by showing me my "core beliefs." Values are just what you hold dear. Beliefs are where you live from, which we will discuss in chapter 7. Next, I was given a book by the female co-lead pastor of the church we were attending. The book, *100 Days of Favor*, was written by Joseph Prince. Lastly, I had gone on cruise and did not have access to anyone outside my family. This meant I had no contact with any of the church leadership for two weeks. This is important because when I came to day 59 of the book and the author stated, "If the enemy can get you to believe the lie that you are not completely forgiven, and keep you sin-conscious, he will be able to keep you defeated, condemned, fearful of God and caught in a vicious cycle of failure." Reading this statement jarred something in me. This statement had reminded me of when I first got saved back at the Baptist church and how I had believed that "all" my sins were forever forgiven. I and the female pastor would always talk about what we were reading. I trusted her, and she had been walking with the Lord longer than I had so I thought she knew more. I could easily be influenced by her to believe something other than what the author had intended. The cruise though prohibited our talking even by email, so I had two weeks of jarring from the Lord without any outside interference. On Sunday, October 26, after I had come back from the family cruise, the Lord prompted me to read about the adulterous woman who was brought to Jesus. Within this story are words I have always struggled with: "Go and sin no more." I struggled with this statement because I would look at what Jesus said and compare it to my life, as a Christian. According to church teaching, I still fell short of living sinless. Jesus told her to go and sin no more...what? My life and this statement from him *did not line up*. Here is what I had written in my journal that day after reading about her again:

> It is a choice to believe, trust, have faith to know you are completely, unconditionally loved by Him. I think when He bent down the second time to write, He was writing who she truly was in Him. He was calling out who she truly is in Him and when she saw that coupled with God's unconditional love and no condemnation she was free. He took all of her sins and had wiped them clean with who she truly is in Him. Notice, He overshadowed what was on the ground and His body fulfilled the law as He wore the tassels. The "disapproval" was covered with "approval."

My perception of God was beginning to change, so it shouldn't be a surprise the next Sunday (November 2, 2014), I woke up and the Lord immediately spoke to me:

"It is time to let go of the rules, Darlene."

In the moment he said this, I understood I needed to let go of a three-hour prayer rule I had been told to comply with by the same female co-lead pastor who had given me the book and I had considered a friend. She had explained the three-hour prayer rule must be adhered to so we could be holy enough, prayed up enough, and in a right relationship with God at all times. This idea, of three hours of prayer, had come from a pastor in South Korea she looked up to because of the miracles, which had been performed in this particular church. She was convinced we must practice this too, so we would be able to perform the same healing miracles at our church. The three-hour prayer would be the ticket to make us holy enough, prayed up enough, and close enough to God to see and experience the same miracles of healing. Every morning I would get up sometimes as early as 3:00 a.m. to pray for the required three hours. Some mornings I would fall asleep, and I would feel guilty; yet God would tell me to "rest."

There were other requirements to being a leader. One of the other "rules" women's leadership was required to follow, if you were married, was to make sure you had sex two to three times a week. I wanted to be "a good wife" and "follow the rules," so I would freak out if we didn't perform our weekly "requirement." The female co-lead pastor was leading from a place of fear. She would tell us our marriage would fail, our husbands would cheat on us, and we would not be living up to our God-given requirement as a wife. My husband works nights and has for years, and we had little kids in the house at the time…now figure out how to "make the requirement." My husband started to push back to this requirement by saying, "If this is a requirement you are just trying to fulfill, forget it." The reason I tell you this is because the Lord used the same exact statement my husband had used for the sex requirement for the three-hour rule. God felt the same way my husband did. God said to me, "Just like your husband wants a real relationship with you and not a box you check off, so do I. I desire intimacy over you just fulfilling your 'time' with me." *Whoa!*

Okay, needless to say *I freaked out* about this! I demanded an explanation from God, "What do you mean, *let go of the rules?*" This *rule* makes me feel *safe*! All of my rules make me feel safe, and they make me feel like *I am doing my part!*" I waited for a response, and all I heard from him was, "It is time to let go of your rules Darlene and rest in me." Needless to say, I finally did listen. I listened because I was exhausted from performing. This began the unwinding of what I had been taught to believe who God is and who I am in him. I had thought I had a relationship with him, but now I began realizing what I had called a relationship was only me trying to perform to make myself appear good enough (religious). I began relearning, with God, how to have a real relationship with him and believing I was already good enough for him.

Little did I realize this was just the beginning of a grand adventure with God. One fraught with pain, heartache, loss, cruelty, lies, hatred, and shunning. Yet, even through all the cruelty at the hands of religious church leadership and Christians, I couldn't let go of God nor what he began showing me. By the end of November, I had spent three days with God that literally began changing my core beliefs, which shifted how I saw God and saw myself. This isn't some new idea. This is actually a two-thousand-year-old idea. Honestly, if we get down to it, this is an idea from the beginning of creation. It is the original idea God had planned since the beginning of time. The mainstream church today has just lost it, but over the last two thousand years, there have been voices bringing the truth back to the forefront to help people truly be free in Christ. To really live and rest in what he lived for, died for, and lives for. What so many people, prior to Christ's coming, had anticipated and desired. I began to realize I was a child again, and God was helping me take off the heavy burden and pick up the light burden in Christ (Matthew 11:30). Are you ready also?

THE DAY I LEARNED GOD HAS ALREADY FORGIVEN ME IT WAS TIME TO FORGIVE MYSELF

I was letting go of the rules, but was there more to all of this? Like most Christians, I believed there was a process I must go through when I sinned or fell short of God's expectations. I had been taught in the church what those expectations are, and I was taught the process I must go through to make sure God would turn his face back toward me and forgive me. I am sure if you have spent any time in the church, you know when you failed to live up to expectations like take every thought captive; do not say the wrong word or have your tongue wag the wrong way; behave kindly; have compassion; show love all the time; be obedient to God; do not lie; do not have a bad thought about someone; do not scream at your kids, husband, family, friends, or neighbors; don't yell at people while driving; do not speed; have sex with your husband two to three times a week; pray for a minimum of three hours; ask what Jesus would do in every situation; and the list went on. If you don't live up to the expectations, then you had to ask God to forgive you for any and all errors you have done or thought. I was taught when I failed in any way in life I needed to ask God to forgive me, wash me of the sinful act, help me not do the same act again, help the people I had hurt, and promise to do better next time—otherwise known as do not sin again. I learned I must either perform perfectly for him 24-7, and if I didn't, I needed to make sure I "repent" to stay in good standing with him, remain close to him, and not have him turn away from me. My belief system was I, because of my bad actions/ choices, had become dirty to God again, and he could not be close to me until I had "repented"; and if I didn't ask for forgiveness/repent, then Jesus's blood would not cover that particular "sin" I had done in word, thought, or deed. If I was unrepentant (this equates to rebellion), this would cause problems for me because God could not come close to help me (because I was dirty to him) until I did ask for forgiveness (aka repent). I was extremely sin conscious and the guilt I felt over my "bad actions or thoughts" would lay there like a huge, heavy blanket; sometimes for years after even when I had already "repented" to God (apologizing to God), and when needed, asked forgiveness from the person I had hurt. I was miserable. My body was hurting everywhere from the stress I was putting myself under, trying so hard to live up to what I had been taught were God's expectations of me and from the guilt of constantly failing at these expectations. I was *exhausted*. Does any of this sound familiar to you? I had put on a heavy yoke God had never intended for humanity to carry. Where was the light burden? Where was the love of God? Didn't he love us before we believed in him, were "clean," or were even "well-behaved"? Why can't he love me now when I make mistakes as a believer? I mean the no-strings-attached kind of love. Agape kind of love. Believing God loved me with no strings attached was not the way I was living my life, nor had I seen any Christians walking around living like this. Does God really love us with no strings attached even after we become "Christians"?

I was about to find out the answer to this question and many more because one Thanksgiving morning four years ago, God met me exactly where I was at. That day and the next two mornings after were going to change everything for me, my family, many friends, and many others who have read my blog. The fateful morning started out simple enough. I had gone to spend some time with God before everyone woke up because I was feeling miserable that morning. Here is where my morning started with an excerpt from my journal, which also included a couple scriptures and a quote:

> "The righteousness which is of the law...does... But the righteousness of faith speaks" (Romans 10:5–6).

"I am the righteousness of God in Christ Jesus" (2 Corinthians 5:21).

"Sin consciousness will draw you to succumb to your temptations, whereas righteousness consciousness gives you the power to overcome every temptation."[1]

Confessing your sins all the time is as if Jesus did not become your sin on the cross.

I wrote: Confessing your sins all the time keeps you sin conscious. It is as if Jesus did not become your sin on the cross. Righteousness consciousness keeps me Jesus conscious. This morning I felt like I had dishonored my mom with some of the words I had spoken. I went into the old mode of asking God to forgive me, wash her, heal her, help her; but I stopped because it wasn't working. The guilt just lay there, and I still felt miserable. So then I said, "I am the righteousness of God in Christ Jesus," and I took my eyes off my behavior and put them on Jesus instead. In this moment, I had a vision (simple enough to say this is like a daydream with God). Here is what I saw and what I understood in this moment:

Some of you might remember when the Dewey decimal file system was used by libraries. For those of you that don't, I encourage you to go and look one up to be able to

---
[1]   Joseph Prince, *100 Days of Favor*, pg. 253.

have an idea of what God was showing me. What I saw though wasn't a small file cabinet but was instead a massive file cabinet, miles high and miles long with individual small drawers. Each drawer had a name written on the outside. As I was standing before this huge cabinet, one of the drawers had my name on it: Darlene Gaston. I pulled open the very long drawer, and it was completely *empty*. I thought, "How can this be?" It was then I understood this drawer had once contained every single sin (all of my sins for my entire lifetime) in word, thought, or deed. This drawer, my account, had been completely emptied for my entire lifetime when I first believed in who Jesus is because of what Jesus had done on the cross. All I did, to have access to this empty drawer, is accept his free gift of righteousness and salvation. This is, was, and will be the place I live from eternally (which means now and forevermore). I understood in this moment I am a new creation in Christ just as Paul had talked about in his letter to the Romans. This was the truth; it had all been finished for me years ago at Cavalry on a Cross. My account was paid in full by Jesus, and there was no longer a payment needed by me. This is the place of truth God wants us all living from. From the truth, we have no account we need to clear because his son has done it all for us when he said, "It is finished." *Wow!* The heavy yoke I had chosen to put on was beginning to loosen and drop away from me in this very moment.

There was still a part of me that had questions though because this heavy yoke had many fibers running through it. All of the puzzle pieces weren't quite fitting together for me yet. My questions were: What about repentance, confession, or forgiveness Lord? How do these words tie in to what you just told me? My understanding of these words did not fit into what he had just shown me. Sometimes when I ask a question, I get a question in reply. Here is what the Lord asked me, "What does repentance mean?" From above, you know what my answer to him was: I need to admit my wrong to you, ask for forgiveness, and renew my promise that I will not do what I did wrong again (which usually failed). He said to me, "Go look up the meaning of repentance," and this is when I became like a child because I had to relearn what I had been incorrectly taught for years. Here is what I found when I looked up the Greek meaning of *repentance* in the Strong's concordance online at biblehub:

To change one's mind; to think after.

"Changing my core beliefs to align with the way God sees things is Repentance"

HBG

In this moment, something happened. I gained wisdom from the Holy Spirit. Before I had understood repentance as coming to God and begging for forgiveness, so he would turn his face back toward me; and if I didn't, he would remain angry at his naughty child, me, until I asked him to forgive me. Now I began to understand what repentance really meant: to change your mind and see things how God sees them. This is how he explained it to me: When Jesus first began his public ministry, he said, "Repent, for the Kingdom of heaven is near." He was letting the Jewish people know there was going to be a major shift in how they saw God. God was not far from them anymore; Jesus was now near them in divine human form. They were going to learn they could never perform all the law in and of themselves; there was only one who could perform all the law and live a perfectly sinless life (Jesus the Son of God); and the Israelites would once again see how much God their father in heaven loves them. A New Covenant was going to be made between God and the whole world. Those who did not either stumble over or think Christ crucified is foolish, would find God (1 Corinthians 1:23). Seeing Jesus and what he did was going to require repentance, especially for the religious elite, the Pharisees and Sadducees.

Because I had the wrong idea about repentance, I now wondered if I had the wrong idea about confess. *Confess* in Greek means:

Agree with God, admit acknowledge.

Yes, I did this. I was really good at acknowledging my wrongs and agreeing with God that I have fallen short when I have. Yet, this had gotten me nowhere except guilt-ridden in the past. I was really good at being "sin conscious," and God wanted me focused on him. Today, as I had tried confessing my wrongs to God, it once again left me wanting. I did not feel like I had been forgiven, which is the same way

I had felt so many times in the past. Before I go further, I want to address something I have heard in the church so many times: "What do feelings have to do with it? You can feel you aren't forgiven but your feelings don't matter." This is not true; God cares very much about our emotions, which we will read about in chapters 7 and 11. Maybe, this time, instead of confessing my wrongs, I needed to confess something different. I remembered I had confessed, "I am righteous in Christ" this morning, and this is when the burden I felt actually lifted——I felt *forgiven*. When we focus on ourselves, confessing all we have done wrong, our eyes are on our abilities or lack of ability. When we focus on what Jesus has done for us instead, we focus on God's abilities. How about agreeing with God (confessing) about what his son has done for us, his love for us, which has no ties to our behavior (good or bad), and he has already forgiven us as we rest in his son? Being able to agree with and acknowledge *all* he and his son have done for us: wiped our slate clean for eternity, come to live inside of us through his Holy Spirit, is taking us from glory to glory, and he desires a close personal relationship with each of us is what God wants us to see, believe, and acknowledge by confession. I feel many churches have missed this extremely important fact. Are we to confess our sins one to another, sure? We ask for forgiveness for those we have harmed. Our relationship with God is different though. When we focus on our ability rather than God's ability, we fall into a religious mindset. This shows we believe our ability is what makes the way for us to be with God (after becoming a believer) rather than believing Jesus is the one who makes the way to God.

When we confess who we are in Christ, we are claiming the gift Jesus died to give us. With this confession, the enemy could no longer keep me focused on what I did wrong. My behavior never made me right with God. Only Christ did. My whole core belief had shifted to what Jesus has done and took the focus off myself. The guilt was no longer there. There was real proof in the pudding, as they say, as I walked away that morning with a real sense of peace.

Because today was Thanksgiving, I needed to get to the turkey; but I had one more word I wanted to look up, *forgiveness*. There were two Hebrew words for *forgive*:

1. *nasa*—taking away, forgiveness or pardon of sin, iniquity and transgression: God's attributes
2. *salah*—God's offer of pardon, forgiveness to the sinner.

In Greek, I found four words that morning:

1. *Aphierri*—to send forth, send away, to remit or forgive debts and sins
2. *Aphesis*—pardon/cancel of punishment
3. *Charizoma*—give, equally remit, forgive pardon
4. *Apoluo*—set free, release, pardon a prisoner, release a debt

This morning I could see from the above definitions, Jesus is either known for or has completed all of them. I began to see a very distinct line between what I call precross and postcross; otherwise known as the Old Covenant (the Law of Moses) and the New Covenant, which was made and sealed in Christ's own blood, his Passover sacrifice on the cross. The New Covenant was made at Golgotha, and there is a distinct time when the covenant of Moses, which are the Ten Commandments, is fulfilled by the only one who could fulfill the law completely for the whole world and for all time (Matthew 5:17). This is Jesus who got up on the cross at Golgotha taking all of our sin on himself because he was the perfect lamb sacrifice (Isaiah 53). Many, like I did, try to live in the New Covenant with Old Covenant requirements, not realizing there is a distinct line between the two. I was beginning to see we can't live in both the Old and the New Covenant.

From this day forward, I began to learn how much God loves me as I sit in this place of grace. Because of my relationship with him, I know he already knows what is in my heart. So, even though I may not say something, he knows I am already thinking it and still it is forgiven. I have this sense of peace now because I know he loves me *no matter what*, even when I may be messy and have terrible thoughts or deeds. When I began to realize I was already forgiven by my Father in heaven, it became so much easier to forgive myself, which leads to being able to forgive others.

I want to finish this chapter with a story. I had a friend who would tell her children they could not stick out their tongue but told them if they felt the need to stick their tongue out they should instead stick their lower lip out. This meant they looked like they were pouting instead of talking back. I, on the other hand, let my kids stick their tongue out. I wanted to know what was in their heart so we could process it out together: the good, the bad, and the ugly. I wanted to help them with their feelings, thoughts, wants, needs, and desires. I wanted to be a part of it all even when it got messy and hard. This is how I parented. I didn't want to pretend or fake it because we can never deal with the real stuff. Like Jesus said, it isn't the outside of the cup we need to cleanse but the inside. Far too often in church or in Christian circles, it is the outward appearance, or behavior, which is focused on rather than the inside of the person. God has always been more concerned with the inner person, our heart. Many Christians live the way my friend taught her kids to act. They feel one way, try to fake the way they feel by redirecting/controlling their feelings, actions, and behavior; but sooner or later, the insides do come bursting out. The Lord showed me when we do this or teach people to do this we end up being strangled, squeezed so tight you can't even breathe. This is when the burst occurs from trying to perform or fake it 'til they make it. Either the physical bodies have symptoms of stress, they act out in hidden ways or just get mean. Anyone ever see some mean Christians out there? I think it is because they are trying so hard to "fake it 'til they make it" just like sticking out your lip instead of your tongue. God though already sees all of you the good, the bad, and the ugly and still loves you with no strings attached. Like I did as a parent, he desires even more to process through all these things with us. He is not condemning us, mad at us, or even expecting us to apologize for our thoughts or behaviors over and over again. He loves us unconditionally and just wants to help us, be there with us through the good times, tough times, and mediocre times. He just wants us.

REALIZING GOD LOVES
ME NO MATTER WHAT

On Thanksgiving Day, I had shared what I had learned with my family. Freedom was coming to our household. I was still in a state of shock and kept wondering if all of this was real. Is it *true*? I couldn't believe this could be true: All my sins forgiven for all time. I didn't have to grovel with God when I did something wrong, even when I wasn't obedient, or if I forgot to do something. I actually woke up that morning feeling so much lighter. It was surreal, and it was scary all at the same time because I felt like I was going against almost one thousand years or more of teaching. I started this day asking God many questions: Is this real? Am I just making this up? And could this really be this easy, this good, and this free? Who am I that God would share or reveal this to and even more why?

I think because the church, as a whole, has made listening or hearing God so difficult, we fail to realize God is always speaking with us, to us. He desires for *everyone* to know, understand, and live from the fact he loves speaking with us. No particular person is more holy, can hear better, or sits at a higher level causing them to hear God better than you can. I am not special… I was just simply ready to hear what he had to say and then he not only asked me to write about it but also gave me the ability to. This is not some new teaching or theology. This is simply coming back full circle to the original teaching of Jesus and his early apostles.

This morning I began with this scripture:

> For you see your calling, brethren, that not many wise according to the flesh, not many mighty, not many noble, are called. But God has chosen the foolish things of the world to put to shame the wise, and God has chosen the weak things of the world to put to shame the things which are mighty. (1 Corinthians 1:26–27)

Then I wrote down what I think the world sees as my weaknesses: my womanhood, my challenge of memorizing, and there are so many more that it would probably take pages to write down.

Weaknesses come in the form of "sin" many times… lying, stealing, looking at pornography, not keeping your word, cheating on your husband or wife in thought or deed, and the list could go on. I was once again on a quest to understand more words today I had questions about. Did I understand what they really meant? I started with *sin* in both the Hebrew and Greek. There are three Hebrew words for *sin* in the Old Testament:

1. *Avon* (ah-vone): iniquity—weakness, or tendency to fall under temptation in specific areas, but does not involve taking action in a condoning way; based on the thoughts, emotions that we know are evil.
2. *Hatah* (ha-tah): transgression—the action of violating God's principles; making a mistake, picking yourself up, and seeing it as God sees it.
3. *Peshah* (pe-shah): sin—deflection or rebellion; to make a counter covenant, deliberate sin consciously choosing to violate God's principles and identifying with the principles of evil in a clear act of rebellion.

In the New Testament, the Greek word *hamarte* is used interchangeably for all three Hebrew words for transgression, iniquity, or sin.[2] *Hamarte* is defined as:

> Missing the mark; making a decision without faith

---

[2] John Klein and Adam Spears, *Devils and Demons and the Return of the Nephilim*, loc: 2183 (digital copy).

Immediately the Lord said to me, "Isaiah 53." I would suggest you go take a look at the entirety of Isaiah 53; but here is what it says in part:

> Surely our griefs He Himself bore, And our sorrows He carried; Yet we ourselves esteemed Him stricken, Smitten of God, and afflicted. But He was pierced through for our **transgressions**, He was crushed for our **iniquities**; The chastening for our well-being fell upon Him, And by His scourging we are healed. All of us like sheep have gone astray, Each of us has turned to his own way; But the LORD has caused the **iniquity** of us all To fall on Him.
>
> But the LORD was pleased To crush Him, putting Him to grief; If He would render Himself as a guilt offering, He will see His offspring, He will prolong His days, And the good pleasure of the LORD will prosper in His hand. As a result of the anguish of His soul, He will see it and be satisfied; By His knowledge the Righteous One, My Servant, will justify the many, As He will bear their **iniquities**. Therefore, I will allot Him a portion with the great, And He will divide the booty with the strong; Because He poured out Himself to death, And was numbered

with the **transgressors**; Yet He Himself bore the **sin** of many, And interceded for the **transgressors**. (Isaiah 53:4–6, 10–12; NASB [emphasis mine])

Here was the "proof" for me right there in Isaiah! Or maybe more like reassurance of what God had shown me yesterday: Jesus took care of all sins, all transgressions, and all iniquities for me and the whole world for our entire lifetime. Jesus took it all upon himself, and it pleased the Father to cause his own son to bear our sins, transgressions, and iniquities. This is *amazing love* and forgiveness. I could really believe, "Sin has no hold upon me." I was beginning to understand the totality of what Christ had done. I am not saying my behavior was perfect; I am saying that *sin has no hold on me*, which really means nothing I do can separate me from God *ever* because of Jesus. I understood my behavior did not dictate whether or not God loved me and forgave me. Jesus's act upon the cross not only proves God's love for me, but also proves the fact I am fully forgiven in Christ for all time. I was beginning to realize that there was nothing I could ever do that would turn the face of my Heavenly Father away from me. I sat in the place of full forgiveness all of the time, no matter what I did or didn't do. This is where Jesus has placed me because of what he had done. I wasn't just saying it but believing this as truth from my most inner self.

Now, anytime a song comes on in which God's goodness is mentioned or even within some secular songs where you know there is a message from God about his goodness,

I can no longer hold back my tears as I cry out for the amazing love and forgiveness my Father and his son had, has, and will continue to have for me and so many others. This is the *real good news*! By the end of day 2, I was grasping the fact God loves me no matter what, the shackles were coming off, and I was further out of the self-imposed prison.

GOD RECONCILES ME TO HIM—NOT THE OTHER WAY AROUND

It is the third day, a Saturday. I think God loves talking to us in numbers, and three is a great number. Jesus's resurrection was in three days and today, like Christ, I felt this was a day of resurrection for me. The false belief had died and the new truth filled belief took its rightful place. After this final day, for me and my family, there was no turning back to the old way of believing. We couldn't. For me if I had turned back it would be like the dog returning to his own vomit or the fool returning to his own folly (Proverbs 23:8). Things were drastically changing for both me and my family. As I continued to share with them what God was showing and telling me, our view of God, his kingdom, and ourselves were changing for the better; we were fully coming into the New Covenant to stay. This morning, I had started with writing the following in my journal:

> We are tormented because we believe
> a lie and pass it down as truth.

The puzzle pieces were beginning to fit correctly as God continued to lay a foundation to rebuild my core beliefs on "His Firm Foundation." After I had written the above statement down, God asked me, "Did you not desire to know me as I know you?" I answered, "Of course, Abba, I have prayed this for years." God's desire is for us to see as him clearly as he sees us (1 Corinthians 13:12). This is exactly what he had been doing with me the last couple of days and would continue to do for the rest of my life; but for today, there were two more words I needed to look up:

1. *Reconciliation*—an exchange; used many times in the past as an exchange of coins. In terms of relationship it means to change from enemies to friends.
2. *Conviction*—the act of convincing.

The scripture which references the first of the two words above:

> For if **while we were enemies we were reconciled to God through the death of His Son, much more, having**

been reconciled, we shall be saved by His life. And not only this, but **we also exult in God through our Lord Jesus Christ, through whom we have now received the reconciliation.** Therefore, just as through one man sin entered into the world, and death through sin, and so death spread to all men, because all sinned... But the free gift is not like the transgression. For if by the transgression of the one the many died, much more did the grace of God and the gift by the grace of the one Man, Jesus Christ, abound to the many.

For as through the one man's disobedience the many were made sinners, even so through the obedience of the One the many will be made righteous. (Romans 5:10–12, 15, 19; NASB [emphasis mine])

In the first bolded section above you can see while we were still enemies, we were reconciled to God through the death of his son. The free gift is made available to us (God's enemies) by God, through his son Jesus because we are saved by his life (how he lived here). We are still God's enemy at this point in the scripture because Paul stated: "While we were enemies we were reconciled to God." The second bolded section states we exult (we boast, we rejoice) in God by coming to the other side (God's side), and now we are friends because we consider him our Lord Jesus

Christ (who is the Word), we are able to come to the other side (God's side) and receive (remember the empty drawer) the reconciliation (friendly relations) because of what God through his son provided for us (emphasis mine). When I better understood what Paul was saying, I realized I didn't have to do anything for God to receive or love me except welcome him as Lord in my life, accepting what he had freely done for me.

The scripture for the second word, *conviction*, is found in John 16:8–11 when Jesus is explaining to his disciples why he has to leave. Jesus was letting them know he would need to leave so he could send the helper, the Holy Spirit to come to them. Jesus states:

> And He, when He comes, will convict the world concerning sin and righteousness and judgment; concerning sin, because they do not believe in Me; and concerning righteousness, because I go to the Father and you no longer see Me; and concerning judgment, because the ruler of this world has been judged. (John 16:8–11, NASB)

The word *convict* is *elegrei* in Greek, and it means "to reprove," which means "to convince." So let's walk through this scripture:

> "And He (the helper, Holy Spirit), when He comes, will convince the world

(the whole of mankind) of sin (self-originated [self-empowered] nature, i.e., it is not originated or empowered by God—comes from lack of belief in him—see next statement), because they DO NOT BELIEVE in ME; and concerning righteousness (he gave us his righteousness through his death on the cross/we are righteous in Christ Jesus—see next statement), because I GO TO THE FATHER; and concerning judgement (not judgement toward mankind but toward the ruler of this world, Azazel whom all sin is attributed to, see next statement), because THE RULER OF THE WORLD HAS BEEN JUDGED."

Jesus, while he walked on earth, made it clear to the Jewish people they could not perform the law perfectly in thought and deed 24-7. If Jesus was letting the Jewish people know they could not perform the full requirements of the law, then I am very sure the Gentiles (you and I) can't either. It is simply not humanly possible. There is only one divine human who came to earth by choice, who completely fulfilled the law, and was the perfect, sinless, divinity in human form sacrifice. This is Jesus, not us.

By faith, I received his free gift of forgiveness, salvation, and reconciliation with the Father; making me a new creation in him. Jesus, on the cross, made the full payment for me for all of my sins and mistakes I have made and will make. I agree or come into covenant with God by believing Jesus has already paid the price for it all for me. I actually began to understand how I could enter into his gates with thanksgiving and his courts with praise (Psalm 100:4). On this third day, God did something for me. I had always been scared of the verse in Matthew 6:14–15 where Jesus says:

> For if you forgive others for their transgressions, your heavenly Father will also forgive you. But if you do not forgive others, then your Father will not forgive your transgressions. (NASB)

This day, I understood this is a prayer Jesus had given to the Jewish people under the Old Covenant. This prayer had to fulfill the law under the Old Covenant. In the New Covenant, there are no requirements for us to find forgiveness from our Heavenly Father. Now, as believers in Christ, we rest in forgiveness—always. This is where we all in the New Covenant need to have a distinct line of Old Covenant (precross) and New Covenant (postcross). With this new understanding, the Lord gave me a vision I would like to finish this chapter with:

I had seen all of the people I had told they needed to forgive someone; otherwise their father in heaven wouldn't forgive them. I realized I had done them an injustice with this by forcing them back under the Old Covenant. There was one particular woman who was standing in the front of all these people. I vowed in this moment if I ever have an opportunity to ask her forgiveness or any of the others, I will.

I then asked the Lord, "What do I do with this? How do I fix this?" and he said to me, "I have this, Darlene. It is covered and finished." In this moment, great peace and gratitude washed over me. I had the experience of knowing within my core being, I am a fully forgiven person who is unconditionally loved by my father in heaven. I was no longer just giving lip service by saying God loved me, but I was beginning to really walk out my life in this belief.

CORE BELIEFS

The foundation of our belief system is so important. Our belief system is actually where we live from, and I call this belief system core beliefs. Our belief system is built up of words. We daily use words to describe how we feel, what we want, what we need, and what we are thinking. Words also hold the way to communicate what one believes or doesn't believe.

Because words are so important to describe what is going on in us, through us, and around us, I would want to make sure my students in my World History class would understand what our topic of the day really meant. As a teacher, one of the things I would do is have a word or words that described our topic for the day, and I would write them on the board. The students then would come up to the board and write down, from their own understanding, how they would define the word or words. Next, I would have my students look up the word in the dictionary; yes, SIRI was asked many times. One of my rules for finding the definition is the word being defined could not be used in the definition, i.e., "religion: the state of the religious." If the word was used in the definition, they would have to dig further and get the deeper meaning or a better understanding of the definition. Through this process, my students soon realized what they thought a word meant wasn't always the same as its definition.

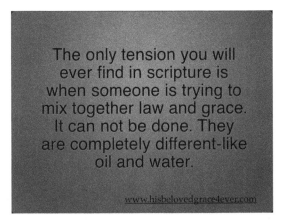

The only tension you will ever find in scripture is when someone is trying to mix together law and grace. It can not be done. They are completely different-like oil and water.

www.hisbelovedgrace4ever.com

So, where am I going with all of this? From the previous chapters, we see God laying a foundation of words he helped me define, just like I had with my students. Like my students, I had thought I understood certain words, which had formed my belief system about God. When God intervened and asked me to look further and dig for the meaning of the words, it opened scripture for me where many times before scripture was too hard to understand, seemed complicated, or there seemed to be two opposing statements from God. Many in the church teach the opposing statements mean there is "tension" in scripture. The only tension you will ever find in scripture is when someone is trying to mix law and grace or the Old and New Covenant together. It cannot be done. They are completely different—like oil and water. If I believed there were two opposing statements in scripture (tension), this would mean I had a wrong perspective of the New Covenant (trying to mix the law and grace). If I had the wrong perspective, then what was the right perspective? What God had begun with me in the three days, he continued doing with me. My perspective became clearer as the definition of words became clearer. This clarity corrected my perspective of scripture, which in turn cleared up my view of God, Jesus, Holy Spirit, myself, and others.

What I found interesting is photographers also like to "correct perspective" in their photos. They need to use

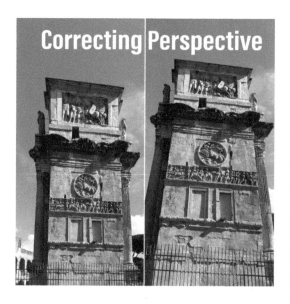

the correct lens to get either the right perspective or a specific distortion in their photo to use this to their advantage in the final outcome of their photo. I, being an amateur photographer (only using an iPhone), had no idea about this ability. I just knew many times what I saw in real life and what the photo looked like were very different. I found when the camera lens was tilted up or down this can cause a totally different perspective in the photo. God, just like photographers do, wanted to correct my perspective. The lens I saw God through were a multitude of words, which built my belief system and filtered the way I saw him. When certain words are incorrectly understood, this would distort or give me the wrong perspective of God. He wanted me to see him clearly, and for this to happen, he needed to be my teacher, like I was to my students. He was going to bring up several words, have me define them, and then go look them up. God wants to make sure our lens is giving us the right perspective to see him clearly. Our lens are the words that make up what I call our core beliefs.

The only book I have read on the subject of "core beliefs" was a requirement for my continuing education as a teacher. Something that landed in my lap as required reading but helped me understand core beliefs enough to explain them. The title of the book is, *Teaching Redemptively* by Donovan L. Graham. In this book, Graham explains the meaning and the difference of core beliefs, which he terms as "controlling beliefs" versus "professed beliefs." The controlling beliefs (which I term core beliefs) is where we actually live our lives from; hence, Graham's word choice of "controlling beliefs." These controlling beliefs are how we see the world, God, people, and ourselves. We make daily choices or formulate our view from these controlling beliefs. What is interesting is what we profess is our belief does not always line up with our controlling/core belief. The way we act though always shows us what our core belief really is, what we truly believe, and how we really see things. There are times when our actions are different than what we say we believe.

One of my favorite examples of this is when I would say, God loves me. I would say this as a professed belief, but my core belief came through in my actions. This means I would state God loves me to people and myself; but my actions would say God only loves me as long as I pray long enough, repent for everything, love him with all my strength and be obedient to him at all times. I mean all of this sounds good, but understand his love for me depended upon my actions and this isn't true because he first loved us even while we were yet sinners (Romans 5:8). Many in the church and many teachers teach one thing yet their actions show something very different. Like me, their core beliefs do not line up with their professed beliefs, so the cycle continues as one generation learns from another within the church.

Donovan also outlines how all humans actually learn, at all ages. He calls it "process content learning." Process content learning involves the cerebral, emotions, and well-being of a person. Process content learning means that a person *experiences* what they learn. What we find throughout most society (in most schools, churches, homes)

- Verbal learning-only speaking, memorization of information-involves only the cerebral cortex of a human

- Process content learning-includes experience, watching, and listening-involves the whole person=emotions, well-being and cerebral cortex (I consider this your spirit, soul, and body learning)

is the form of verbal teaching that expects people to verbally learn. We have all experienced this type of teaching and learning. At school, we would listen to the teacher drone on about a subject or read a book about a subject and then we would be expected to verbalize it again either out loud in class, in a written paper, or on a test. Because verbal learning only involves the cerebral part of the person, we can regurgitate the information; but this does not mean we have taken this information as a part of our core beliefs. Process content learning, on the other hand, because it involves the whole person (spirit, soul, body), impacts the cerebral, emotions, and well-being of a person. Process content learning is happening all the time as we watch people we trust or the people we look up to (mentors, teachers, parents, pastors, etc.) as they walk out their lives. This is actually how our core beliefs are formed by our experiences. Our core beliefs are where we make our choices from; we do not make our choices from our professed beliefs.

Process content learning with our whole being far outweighs verbal learning in everyone's life. This is how God created us. I can attest to this fact. I personally learned, acted, and made personal choices in my own Christian walk more by watching other Christians than any sermon I had listened to. Don't get me wrong, I could write notes and repeat some of what was taught on Sunday. I spoke what sounded good but my choices, my life, my actions didn't bear out what I spoke all the time. As I watched other Christians, I formed many core beliefs that did not line up with God's truth. What I found were many of my choices and actions were fear-based because I did not really know who God is and who I am in him within my core. What I would *say* I believed and what I really believed and *acted on* could be different depending upon what I had process content learned, as I watched other Christians that I trusted, held in esteem, believed had more knowledge than myself, or I considered as teachers. I want to make it clear I am not talking about good and bad behavior, but instead am talking about my professed beliefs about who God is and who I am in him and my core beliefs differing. God wanted to correct my perspective of him and have my professed beliefs match my core beliefs. This would allow me to walk out what I say I believed, cause me to see him for who he is, and see myself for who I am in him. This is exactly what he wants for everyone.

The biblical story God had given me to help me better understand process content learning with him is the short story of Simon of Cyrene. Simon would bear the cross for Jesus on part of the walk to Golgotha. The cross can signify a multiplicity of spiritual meanings. At this time, the Lord wanted me to see how the cross signified the law for the Jewish people. Jewish law required death to those who blasphemed God, but the Jews could not act on their own at this time in history. Instead the Jewish high priests had to take their case to Pontius Pilate who ruled this area under the Roman Empire. The Roman empire's law did allow for crucifixion for those not following the Roman law. Both the Romans and Israel high priests were using the cross to fulfill their law.

Another significant part of this story is a small Greek word placed within the verse that starts our story. The

Greek word is *pherin*, which means "carry or bear" and is found in only two scriptures in the New Testament. The first time is in the start of our story in Luke 23:26 and the second time is in John 15:4, which we will talk about in a moment. First, Luke 23:26:

> When they led Him away, they seized
> a man, Simon of Cyrene, coming in from
> the country, and placed on him the cross
> to **carry** behind Jesus. (NASB)

In these times you could not deny a Roman soldier his request; so Simon begins to carry the cross, the very instrument which signified the Jewish law, behind Jesus through the town to Golgotha. It is dusty, hot, and people are lining the walk shouting, crying, or maybe even trying to mind their own business. The cross was heavy, and carrying it was probably difficult and exhausting; but Simon, following Jesus, carried the cross all the way to Golgotha. Once Simon reaches Golgotha, he then puts the cross down because his job is done. If this were me, in this moment, I would be thankful I was not the one who would have to go further and actually be crucified. We don't know if Simon watched the rest of what unfolded, but we do know Jesus completely embraces the cross and what will be done to him. The embracement of what would be done to him, I believe, began the night before when he had wept tears of blood and told his father, "Not My will but Yours" (Luke 22:42). Jesus laid his body, of his own free will, on top of the cross; he is nailed to it; bleeds on and into it, and then the cross is raised up. Do you see how Jesus covers the law with himself and is the perfect sacrifice that both fulfills and covers the law?

This story helps us visualize the meaning of process content learning. Nothing is said that we know of between Simon and Jesus. Yet, the unspoken, the actual doing/actions/decisions, is what has the most impact on humans in their ability to learn something. This is what forms our core beliefs and affects our actions and choices in life.

Simon experienced this type of learning as he carried the weight and burden of the law upon his back, which the cross represented. Simon laid the cross down at Golgotha and Jesus embraced it. Simon even if he was a good man, he could never fulfill what Jesus could. One last significant piece of information I found is many historians believe Simon may have been both Jewish and Gentile. This would be just like God to add an important detail, which signifies all people were redeemed that day. A fact which would come out later with Peter's clean and unclean vision he had on a rooftop (Acts 10:9–16). God was making clear, through the symbolism of one person, his intent for all people to have the ability to lay their burden, their inability, their lack, their sin, their need to perform the law at Golgotha just as Simon had stopped carrying the cross there and handed it over to Jesus.

I believe what happened to Simon during this short but powerful time is he realized outside of Jesus he could not carry, bear, or do what was going to be required of Jesus to do. I believe as Simon carried the cross behind Jesus, Simon followed Jesus keeping his eyes on the only one who could truly do *all* things. Jesus is the one who is spotless; there was no sin found in him. He was the holy sacrificial lamb, and firstborn son of God.

This is where the second verse, which contains the Greek word *pherin*, which gives us the ability to see God's full picture. People, both inside and outside of the church building, want to "know," "find," or "fix" themselves. We try to find out who we are or fix ourselves to be better Christians by being introspective of ourselves either apart or with Jesus. Introspection though isn't what he asked us to do. This is a human desire not God's, so it fails. We find out introspection is far too difficult and far too weighty for us. But there is one who can and wants to help us. The answer to "finding ourselves" is right in the second "pherin" scripture found in John 15:4:

> Abide in Me, and I in you. As the branch cannot **bear** fruit of itself unless it abides in the vine, so neither can you unless you abide in Me. (NASB)

As we abide in Jesus and he in us, we find out who we are. Abiding simply means: waiting, remaining for a long time, a lifetime. We are a branch, which is attached intertwined with the vine. Just look at a plant and see how one ends and the other begins, yet they are one. The branch knows how it needs the vine because if the branch is cut off, it doesn't survive, but the vine will survive. As I abide in Jesus and he is in me I become one with him. With this oneness I naturally, over time, become the best version of myself. As we let go of the belief we have to perform and instead abide, as the branch does with the vine, our eyes focus more readily on what Jesus did for us, remembering his sacrifice and where this places us. This focus shifts our eyes from our behavior to Jesus's behavior; our need to make ourselves better to his sacrifice, which makes us a new creation, and our attempt at righteous behavior to him proclaiming us as righteous. I believe this is one of the reasons Jesus implemented the Eucharist. To symbolize him living in us through the act of eating the bread (his body) and drinking the wine (his blood). (More in chapter 10.)

Simon's experience is exactly what Graham called "process content learning." The "process content learning" happens naturally within us as we abide in Jesus, we learn with our whole being. As believers, because God is living inside of us through his Holy Spirit, we are constantly "process content learning" with the best teacher we could ever ask for.

I was able to also see how Jesus had taught by process content learning throughout his walk here on earth and how he does this with us now as we abide/rest in him. Even when we have sinned, as a believer, we still abide in him because: "We walk in the Light as He Himself is in the Light, we have fellowship with one another, and the blood of Jesus His Son cleanses us from ALL sin" (1 John 1:7 NASB). This means we walk in the Light, who is Jesus, by faith-believing that Jesus is your Lord and Savior because "He made Him who knew no sin to be sin on our behalf, so that we might become the righteousness of God in Him" (2 Corinthians 5:21, NASB).

Our behavior does not qualify us.
Christ's behavior qualifies us.

This is where we are seated at all times no matter of our right or wrong behavior. Our behavior isn't what qualifies us, it is Christ's behavior, which qualifies us and gives us righteousness. Because I rest in him and all he has done for me, as a branch I bear fruit naturally. It is not something I am trying so hard to produce like I had in the past. A branch rests on the vine and naturally produces fruit. The branch doesn't work hard to produce fruit; it just can't help itself because it is attached to the vine. I am constantly because I abide in the vine (Jesus), bearing fruit. Do I always appear to be bearing fruit? Oh no. I understand now, this life is a process of going from glory to glory with a lot of messes in the mix from my own choices; but I know He still loves me in the middle of all of the good, the bad, and the ugly. Here is an example, which helped explain how abiding in him works:

Have you ever noticed after spending a lot of time with someone, it could be a husband, wife, parent, sibling, friend, you pick up some of their mannerisms? You may not have even noticed it, but others do. You may have noticed when siblings, family, or friends get together how their actions, looks, or laughs can be the same. They have simply lived life together for a while and have picked up one another's mannerisms. Well, this is exactly what it is like when we abide in Jesus, when we keep our eyes focused on him and off of ourselves. This is what it means to naturally bear fruit in Jesus. There is no striving, it comes naturally.

It is only natural to grow by "process content learning" with Jesus in you. This is why Paul stated in 2 Corinthians 3:18, "But we all, with unveiled face, beholding as in a mirror the glory of the Lord, are being transformed into the same image from glory to glory."

COME OUT OF THE CAVE
INTO A WIDE OPEN FIELD

In the weeks and years that followed the initial three days with God came moments of scripture popping up in my mind or hearing someone say something, which did not fit my new viewpoint of God. God used these times to show me my old belief system and help me change my core beliefs to match his truth. One of the first scriptures God and I tackled together is from Hebrews 11:6:

> Without faith it is impossible to please God. (NASB)

The word *faith* is *pistis* in Greek. *Pistis* means belief, trust. The word *please* here is fully defined as "pleasure" from the Greek. So you could say instead:

Without trusting God it is impossible to give God pleasure. (Emphasis and further definition added is mine from Strong's Concordance at biblehub)

I had always thought my behavior is what pleased God; but here in the letter to Hebrews, it really stated I needed to trust God to please him. Our performance is not what brings us closer to God. The Hebrews needed to understand this as they had, for centuries, lived acting, thinking, and believing their performance is what pleased God. This is because they lived under the Old Covenant law for centuries. The Hebrews, like many of us in the church today, needed to hear we can either live free by trusting/believing Jesus has accomplished all he said he did, or we choose to live trusting/believing God requires good behavior on our part so we can remain in our salvation, freedom, and holiness. The latter choice puts ourselves back under the law, living a heavily burdened life of requirements to perform our best and keep up what we think we "owe" God. God didn't plan for us to work for any part of our salvation; why would he have sent his son then? Yet, I find a large portion of the "churches" teach us by their behavior the law mixed with a little grace rather than just grace. Paul made it clear to the Romans: By Grace we are saved; not by our works (yes, we will discuss faith without works in chapter 10). Works along with a yearly sacrifice to God is what *had to be performed* under the covenant of Moses. Now, we live under the covenant of Jesus, which declares: all has been done for us to make us right with God and he was the ultimate sacrifice for all time, for all people.

I used to say I understood and knew all he had done, but I didn't. I had one foot in the New Covenant and one foot in the Old Covenant. God wanted me entirely living in the New Covenant, and he wants the same for you.

John the Baptist had the same exact problem we have today, one foot in the Old Covenant and one foot trying to find itself in the New Covenant. John had a tough job. He knew who Jesus was, and he saw what Jesus was doing, but John's core beliefs were firmly set in the Old Covenant because of how he had grown up. John had even proclaimed, "Repent!" but still had a tough time seeing how things were going to change. John was the last of the Old Testament prophets and what he had process content learned throughout his life was a stumbling block for him. Like many today, who have process content learned in the church, to have one foot in the Old Covenant and one foot in the New Covenant; Jesus has become a stumbling block for them. Let's begin with what Jesus said about John in Matthew 11:11–13, NKJV:

> Assuredly, I say to you, among those born of women there has not risen one greater than John the Baptist; but he who is least in the kingdom of heaven is greater than he. And from the days of John the Baptist until now the kingdom of heaven suffers violence, and the violent take it

by force. For all the prophets and the law prophesied until John. (Matthew 11:11–13 NKJV)

I have heard this verse taught so many different ways, yet I have never felt settled with what I was being told. I have also read a great translation of it from Greek to Hebrew to English, but still didn't feel like I understood it. Now, I was beginning to see God for who he is I was finally able to understand what this scripture meant.

First, let's look at a translation of words from the above verse from excerpts in the book, *Jesus the Jewish Theologian*[3]:

> As we will see, instead of "suffers violence" [Matthew 11:12] the action words "the kingdom of heaven breaks fourth" are much closer to the real meaning of the text... This translation of biazō is more appropriate than the passive idea from "suffers violence" because the active meaning correctly conveys both the force associated with the verb and also mentions the progressive movement of the divine reign. At times, the Hebrew verb paretz, which means "to break forth" was translated by the Greek verb biazō in the Septuagint. The idea conveyed by the Greek verb certainly includes the action of breaking out with strong force... Unquestionably, the

---

3 Brad H. Young, *Jesus the Jewish Theologian*, pgs. 51–55.

entire saying of Jesus [above scripture] is connected to the words of the prophet Micah:

He who opens the breach (the breaker, haropetz) will go up before them; they will break through (partzu) and pass the gate, going out by it. Their king(malkam) will pass on before them, the Lord at their head. (Micah 2:13)

The Hebrew word radaf is best translated as "to pursue earnestly"... The text [Matthew 11:12] could be translated into Hebrew, mega me yochanan hamatbil vead atah malchut shamayim poretzet vehaportzim rodfim [mevakshim] otah, "From the days of John the Baptist until now, the kingdom of heaven breaks forth and those breaking forth are pursuing [seeking] it." This translation brings out the meaning of the Greek text. The concept conveyed by this translation of the verse in Matthew would be similar to the words of Psalm 34:14, "seek peace and pursue it" (bekesh shalom verodfehu)... The essence of Matthew 11:12 dynamically portrays the ones breaking out of the sheepfold. They actively pursue the divine purposes in life..."

The above definitions, which clarify the meaning of the Greek and Hebrew help give us a deeper understanding to what was stated by Jesus. But this alone did not help me, my perspective of God had become clearer, which enabled me to finally see what was really being said. This clarity not only gives a rich and beautiful picture of who Jesus is, but also gives a better picture of what John the Baptist was thinking while he sat in jail sending his disciples to question Jesus. Here is how God explained this to me:

John the Baptist was the "breaker" Elijah who had been written about and would come before the Messiah. I see Elijah as the opening or partition between the last of the "law prophets" and the new covenant "grace prophets." John the Baptist expected and believed because he grew up under the Old Covenant. Jesus had come to judge the world at this time. We know this is John's belief because when John first began his ministry he stated: "His winnowing shovel (fork) is in His hand to thoroughly clear and cleanse His [threshing] floor and to gather the wheat and store it in His granary, but the chaff He will burn with fire that cannot be extinguished" (Luke 3:17, AMP).

What John saw Jesus do versus what John had said Jesus had come to do was causing confusion for John. At this time, the expectation for the followers of Jesus were he would take his rightful place on the throne here on earth, overthrow the Roman rule, and bring the Jewish people peace on earth. This would be accomplished here by throwing the chaff (the mean and evil people who did not follow Jehovah) into the fire. When John was thrown into prison and Jesus was not "making these things happen" like John said he would, he began to have some serious questions. This is when John sent his disciples to question Jesus. Here is what Jesus told him:

> And blessed (happy, fortunate, and to be envied) is he who takes no offense at Me and finds no cause for stumbling in or through Me and is not hindered from seeing the Truth. (Matthew 11:6, AMP)

Jesus was letting John know: He had not come to judge the world, at this time, and John was stumbling over his own perspective he had of Jesus, which was Jesus coming now to judge the world by the law. This judgment, John was seeking to happen, will not occur until the second coming. Jesus was redirecting John to look at the reality of what he was doing right now: healing and restoration; and that this would become a season of grace. John doubted who Jesus was because his perspective was from the *law*. Jesus had to help John see what he was doing now was exactly what was expected of him during this time.

Jesus is known as the door (John 10:2), and he is the only way through to the open grace filled kingdom of heaven living within you. Jesus said, "I am the Door; anyone who enters in through Me will be saved (will live). He will come in and he will go out [freely], and will find pasture" (John 10:9, AMP).

Lastly, I want to share the picture God had given me which will bring further clarity:

Imagine a cave (see picture) and the sheep are following the shepherd into the cave for the night for safety. The law is like the cave. It keeps you safe and protected from the night (the curse). Shepherds know sheep will not jump over even a low wall. Shepherds would put up a low stone wall or even lie down in front of the cave entrance to keep the sheep safe inside. In the morning when the sun rises (Jesus), the shepherd would get up or kick (break) the wall and let the sheep out into the wide open. We are his sheep, he is the gate—the shepherd that put up the wall to keep his sheep safe in the cave (law). This is why the law is not bad, but it can never save you from sin (Romans 7). John the Baptist (watchmen, breaker) broke the wall and the good shepherd (Jesus) has led the way out of the cave (law) and into wide open spaces (grace), and we are no longer confined to the cave (law).

Yet, there are times, we as humans, want/desire to go back into the cave or maybe just stand at the entrance of the cave, part in and part out of the cave. A little grace and a lot of law or more grace and a little law. When we hang around the cave, it puts the millstones around our necks (Mark 9:42), and we can stumble just like John the Baptist was. Jesus told John not to stumble over him. Jesus wants us to fully come out of the cave and no longer have one foot in and one foot out. Jesus is saying, "Come all the way out. It is safer here because of my grace, mercy, and complete forgiveness rests out here in the wide open spaces." Do not go back to even a little of the law because when you do (Galatians 4:21–5:6) you come under the full law and are judged by the law.

Is it scary to live in this wide open space? It was for me at first because when you have lived under the law just a little bit it can seem too free and too good to be true in the beginning. It becomes easier though as I learned to know him for who he is and know who I am in him. God kept reminding me of his great plan and who I am: "The watchman (John the Baptist) opens the door for this man (Jesus), and the sheep (the people who follow Jesus) listen to his voice and heed it, and he calls his own sheep by name and brings (leads) them out. When he has brought his own sheep outside, he walks on before them, and the sheep follow him because they know his voice. They will never [on any account] follow a stranger, but will run away from him because they do not know the voice of strangers or recognize their call (John 10:1–5, AMP).

I finally understood the last "law prophet," John the Baptist, was the breaker that caused the sheep (all of us) to be able to follow our King Jesus into the wide open space of freedom, grace, mercy, and complete forgiveness. Just a little faith…as small as a mustard seed was needed.

FAITH AS SMALL AS A MUSTARD SEED

In the past, I believed I had to muster enough faith to believe in God, please God, see healings, experience healings in myself, and see a multitude of miracles. I questioned, "Exactly how do I do this and how does this work?" and "Do I have enough faith?" I didn't understand how this whole faith thing worked and kept trying within myself to just have enough faith. Many times I was called on to pray for people, and many times I found myself afraid of not "performing" well enough for God, for people, and for the person I was praying for. Many times I found myself thinking and believing: Today, yesterday, this week, or this year, I failed in this area and this area because of these failures I am not good enough for God, he isn't going to hear my prayers and my "faith" for any positive answer to my prayer would sink. Thus this would eat away at my faith and belief God can do anything. With this type of thinking, my core belief "faith," which I had learned from other Christians, was in my behavior and not in God. Thankfully, God stepped in and changed the way I saw things to see the way he sees things (repentance).

From the previous chapter, we learned the definition of faith is:

believe, trusts in, clings to, relies on

To explain the mustard seed, we need to look a little deeper into the scripture in Hebrews 11:6: "Without faith it is impossible to please God."

I discovered, as I dug a little deeper, the sentence was written in a "passive voice," and there is a good reason why this sentence is written in a passive voice. The passive voice helps us understand how God works within us. It reminds us of the very fact: Everything we are able to do comes from him, not ourselves. This means even the ability to have faith, as small as a mustard seed, was planted by him (Matthew 17:20). When we read Hebrews, we need to remember this letter was written to Hebrews (Jewish believers in Jesus Christ). Hebrews, just like John the Baptist, fully understood from childhood as they watched and learned from those around them they need to keep the law and perform a yearly sacrifice because all would fail at keeping the law perfectly. Now we have Jesus, our perfect sacrifice; but the belief system which came from the law: "IF I will, then God will do for me," still lives on right now in our churches just as it was trying to live on with the Hebrews. Many in the church today believe, as the scribes in Jesus's day: The law was there for man to fulfill (Mark 3:28–30). This had been the agreement at Mount Sinai between the Israelites and God. The law created a system, we as humans are very fond of, where we need to perform to receive from God. Humans have this need to try to make ourselves "right." I believe we either try our hardest to make things right with God or we know we can't and just give up. The truth is we can never "make ourselves right enough" for God. It is impossible for us to perform *perfectly every single time* in thought or actions. Paul, in his letter to the Hebrews, was describing how simple faith, in God, has always brought righteousness in the covenant prior to Mount Sinai (read all of Hebrews 11). He also points out that the patriarchs were waiting for the "better way," which we now have through Jesus. Paul was letting the Hebrews know their belief in Jesus, who he is, makes us righteous because of Christ's divine exchange at the cross.

Another interesting point, about passive voice, is English teachers do not like you to write sentences in this form. The reason English teachers steer you away from writing in passive voice is it makes the sentence unclear or it can be misinterpreted. The Lord had me write this verse into an "active voice" sentence, so I could better understand what he was expressing to me. When I read Hebrews 11:6 in the active voice all fear regarding my performance in mustering enough faith to live up to God's expectations disappeared. God is the one who activates everything in us, we freely choose to accept or deny it. Below is the scripture in the active voice:

> "God has pleasure when we believe, trust in, cling to, rely on Him." (Emphasis and further definition added is mine from Strong's Concordance at biblehub)

We do not self-create our faith, ever. Each of us has faith deposited into us by God as small as a mustard seed. This small mustard seed is what first gives us the ability to believe in Jesus, in who he is. All we do is repent (see things differently than before) and see that the kingdom of heaven is here in the person of Jesus. This ability to see things differently is given to each of us by God, the faith as small as a mustard seed. The coinciding of our free will and this seed given by God causes us to see Jesus for who he is, just like the one thief on the cross did. Our free will to say yes to this seed activates the mustard seed into growth and the kingdom of heaven is invited in to break forth in each individual's life.

When the seed is activated to grow, do we as humanity have any part in causing that seed to grow? No, God even takes care of the seed growth. It helps us to remember he is the planter, the pruner, the one we abide in, the solid rock with great soil for us to grow in. We do not prune nor do we produce the right soil. God does. He is the vinedresser, we are not. Nothing we do or don't do qualifies or disqualifies us to accomplish these miracles of faith. We start with the seed God gives us, God is the one whom grows our faith, and he is both the author and finisher of our faith (Hebrews 12:2). Our one and only action, with his help, is using our free will to say yes to him in the very beginning. Greater faith isn't attained by you; it is completed by the father in heaven as you just believe, trust in, cling to, and rely on him as a branch does to the vine.

There is absolutely nothing that stands in your way of Jesus. The only thing which Christ does not do for you is your "free will choice" of seeing Jesus for who he is. Just like the other thief on the cross choose not to believe who he is. He will never force his free gift upon you, but even when you say no to the seed he is still there passionately chasing after you to the very last moment. To him you are the lost lamb he will always leave the other ninety-nine to go and look for (Matthew 18:12).

We have now walked into a wide open space realizing our behavior isn't what brings pleasure to God but our trust in him, and we have discovered where faith really comes from; but I know there is a scripture in the New Testament that speaks about works and faith. Something like, without works you have no faith? What about that?

What Came First the Chicken or the Egg (aka Faith or Trust)?

I can hear the questions because I had the same questions: But what about behavior? And isn't it true faith without works is dead? I think this brings us to the age-old question... What came first the chicken or the egg? It is such a great question. For those of us who believe in creation by an all-powerful creator, then of course we answer the chicken; because in the beginning he formed all the animals out of the dirt (Genesis 1:24). We also were formed from dirt; yet, we were given the image and the breath of God (Genesis 1:27 and Genesis 2:7). Amazing! So, here is another great question: What comes first faith or works?

Many teachers, in the church, when they find what appears to be opposing statements within the Bible, will call it "tension in scripture." Kind of like a yin and yang. For me, it makes God appear bipolar and does not explain to me what is really being said. Now, if I see "tension in scripture," I understand there is a place within my core beliefs holding on to the Old Covenant. This means I am trying to mix the Old and New Covenants together. Which then leads to me trying to work really hard to make God happy. I find when my core beliefs change to the truth of the New Covenant there is no longer "tension in scripture" but instead there is "agreement in scripture." Now that we are getting a more solid foundation of how we see God and see ourselves it is time to get to a more difficult topic.

What does come first then, faith or works? We seem to have to opposing scriptures, one is Hebrews 11:6 from the last chapter and the opposing one would be from James 2:17:

> Thus, faith by itself, unaccompanied by actions, is dead. But someone will say that you have faith and I have actions. Show me this faith of yours without the actions, and I will show you my faith by my actions! (James 2:17–18, NASB)

The reason James is pulled out and pointed to by the religious is because their core belief is "if I will then God will." I believed this way not so long ago, and I wanted my behavior to prove I had Christ living in me. I had to show the world Jesus was really in me! It was something I thought about, worked hard at, and planned for. It was a job for me. I had to prove to God and the world I loved him, had faith, and would be trustworthy with any gifts he gave me. My faith (trust/belief) was actually in "proving God lived in me" instead of in God himself. I trusted more in my behavior and my ability to control my behavior than I did in Jesus and what he was naturally doing inside me. I was putting the cart before the horse in my belief.

This is part of the heavy load or burden I talked about before. Instead of resting in what Jesus has done, is doing, and will do for me I instead was having to perform for God, people in the church, and the world. Not only was this a heavy burden, but if you messed up, which I did frequently, then you begin to think you will never make it as a "good Christian," you are a failure, you are not good enough for God or anyone, God doesn't love you, and if God doesn't love you than neither can your family, your friends... Wow, I can't even love myself. What a terrible cycle to be in. Like a hamster on a wheel, never getting anywhere, except more hopeless. If I am a branch resting in God then what was James saying to the readers of his letter?

Looking at the context of the letter and the Greek words James had used, opens up and clarifies what he was actually saying. In his letter, James uses a specific Greek word *dipsuchos*, which is translated as double-mindedness (James 1:8 and 4:8). *Doubleminded* means "literally: of two souls, of two selves, double-mind-properly, two souled; (figuratively) double-minded, i.e. a person split in half, vacillating like a spiritual schizophrenic." These type of people James was speaking about in his letter were those who had said with their mouth "Jesus is Lord" and yet the outflow of their life showed "something different." The "something different" James spoke of were a desire to treat poor people harshly and rich people well, not taking care of widows and orphans or favoritism of wealthy people in the body of Christ. James called these actions a vulgarity.

People see symptoms
get focused on their behavior
try to find ways to treat their symptoms
never realizing that their symptoms
are caused because of their core beliefs.

James understood there would be an easy, natural outflow of actions when you have faith in Jesus. Last chapter, I spoke of the seed growing into the tree, which is the kingdom of heaven living in and through you and how God is the one who does this through you. This is exactly what James is saying too. When we start with the true core belief, we are saved by grace, then we will understand the works we do are a *natural outflow* of our faith in Christ, which has allowed the Holy Spirit to dwell in us.

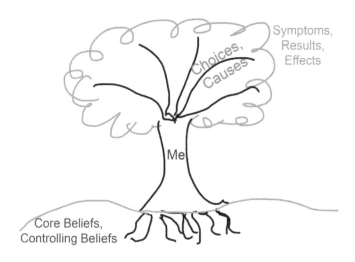

One of the ways God helped me understand all of this is by showing me a vision of a tree. When I saw the tree, he reminded me how symptoms in your body are the leaves of the tree and how we must look at the dirt where the roots (core beliefs) are to see what is going on to cause our symptoms. He reminded me of how our "core beliefs," when not aligned with the truth, we will say one thing but actually believe something entirely opposite, which are shown by our actions (the leaves). Whatever our core beliefs are we act out of them. We may say "God is Sovereign" but then we are shocked and will not believe he would move amongst a group of unbelievers or how could he ever show up outside the four walls of church during a secular song to meet a person right where they are at? He can and will do whatever he wants, when he wants because he is sovereign. One of my favorite stories of God doing this is the video when Hugh Jackman, while practicing singing "From Now On" for the movie *The Greatest Showman*, all of a sudden got his voice back after his surgery. God's Spirit is tangible within this video, and I highly recommend watching this video if you can. Some people try to limit God to their own box, what is comfortable for them, otherwise known as their core beliefs. Our core beliefs can stand in the way of seeing all God is doing in our lives and others. Even when I had brought this revelation to a pastor, who had asked me to know what God had a shown me, he could not or would not see it. His core beliefs stood in the way. He may say one thing but in his core beliefs he didn't believe it. He had the wrong perspective of God. Jesus had become a stumbling block for him. At the end of our first meeting, I had said to him, "The difference in what we believe is: I believe that God will never leave me nor forsake me and you believe God turns His face from you when you sin." His core belief had him with one foot in the Old Covenant and one foot in the New Covenant brought about by his core belief he must perform for God to love him, giving him the wrong view of what Jesus had done for him, which was supported by the belief there is tension in scripture. He was unable to change (repentance) his view of God. This is why core beliefs are so important. We will live from either the correct or the incorrect perspective of God, which impacts every area of our life.

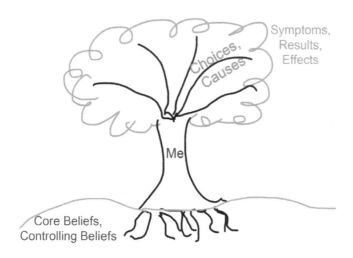

Let's look at the tree again remembering we automatically act out of our core beliefs. Our core beliefs lead us in our "walk," many times without us even realizing or thinking about it, it is automatic…naturally happens. The leaves, in the above picture are the "effects," which most Christians are looking at. These are the outcomes of our choices or the cause and effect in our life. We get caught up with "*sin*" and making sure our leaves don't show any signs of it. We are looking so closely at the leaves we don't actually acknowledge where our roots are really planted or how we have gone back to one foot in the Old Covenant and one foot in the New. I have found Christians so focused on their behavior, trying to find ways to treat their symptoms while never realizing their symptoms are caused because of their wrong core beliefs. Their core beliefs have put the cart before the horse, so the focus is on themselves rather than on Jesus. I used to be so focused on the leaves also; but now I am more interested in my core beliefs lining up with God which puts my focus back on Jesus. When we focus less on the leaves (our behavior) and focus on Jesus we are being the branch attached to the vine rather than trying to be the vine.

I have found either our core beliefs line up with the truth or they line up with our own belief systems we have created out of fear. Instead of reverencing God for what he has done for us, we have become afraid of God. We either believe God first loved us or God only loves us when we behave properly. Our belief system (the roots of the tree) are planted in dirt. This dirt is what feeds our belief system. Either we are planted in the dirt of the law, otherwise known as the tree of good and evil or we are planted in the dirt of grace, which is the tree of life. These are the two trees found within the garden of Eden. One tree (knowledge of good and evil) we ate from through Adam. The other tree (of life) we ate from through Jesus. So many Christians, like I had, start off with the tree of life when they first get saved and then are found running back to the tree of good and evil because this is what we learn to do as we sit in many churches and learn by watching and listening. When we go back to the tree of good and evil, our house is really not been planted on the rock, as Jesus had wanted; but on the shaking, moving sand of our own behavior (Matthew

7:24–27). Our behavior will never line up perfectly with Christ's behavior, ever. We will make mistakes, fumble, do the wrong things…we are simply humans living in a fallen world, who have been given the tree of life as a free gift from our Father in Heaven through the death and resurrection of His Son, Jesus.

Love based on fear Tree of Good and Evil	FEAR	Judged, not good enough, unable to truly love yourself or your neighbor, never measuring up, not content with who you are, sin behavior focused and the list could go on.
Love based on the fact God loves us no matter what "First loved us" Tree of Life	PERFECT LOVE	Free, loved, able to love yourself then you can love your neighbor, cherished, content with who you are, whole, JESUS focused and the list could go on.

In humanity, whether you are a believer or a nonbeliever, you live from either of these two places (reference chart). Unbelievers will fall under the first row. Sadly, we have many, many Christians who first are under the second row and then go back to the first row, like I had said above. We watch other Christians, we look up to, and hear sermons about our need for good behavior for God to love us, which lead us back to the tree of good and evil. We may also have heard if we live entirely under the row of grace we will go down a slippery slope and lose our salvation. Those which hold these core beliefs fall under the first row of fear based living. Do you see how we can only live under one of the two belief systems? We can't do both at the same time, but we can hop from one to the other. When we try to live between the lines of both beliefs we become those double-minded people James speaks of. We say we believe in Jesus, yet we also believe our behavior will in some way add to what Jesus did on the cross. Jesus had asked me, "Haven't I already done enough?" Isn't what he did enough to firmly plant us in the tree of life perspective? I am so grateful for God's intervention in my life with his truth. When we were told to leave our church because I would not stop blogging, people said we were on a slippery slope; and if we haven't yet, we will soon lose our salvation. But I say we found love, and we found our salvation. Do my choices always look perfect, no…but I understand God is the pruner, not myself, and I trust he is going to do a fantastic job in the end with me, my children, and others.

Which dirt you are you going to set yourself in? Our deepest desire, within each of us, is to be unconditionally loved. This is a fact whether we acknowledge it or not. We will not find unconditional love in *fear*, but will always find it in *grace* (1 John 4:18). I will promise you though…if you do choose the second set of beliefs you will be amazed at the leaves you will see being produced. The production will naturally happen within you as you know (believe) within your core you do not need to add anything to what Jesus has done to be accepted, loved, and cherished exactly where you are right now. This is when you begin to really believe and live from the place "God loves me no matter what." This is what it means to be saved by grace.

If we are saved by grace in Christ, then what exactly is *grace*? Divine grace is defined by the Merriam-Webster dictionary as:

> Unmerited, divine assistance given to humans for their sanctification and regeneration; a virtue coming from God; a state of sanctification coming from God.

The Greek word for *grace* is *xaris* and is defined as:

> "extension towards," "free gift" undeserved favor. The core idea is God's extension towards man, a favor or freely extending Himself to give Himself away to people. The idea is His favor/Grace is extending towards people because He is inclining/reaching because He is **disposed** to bless them. This Greek word is closest to the Hebrew word kana=favor, grace, elegance, charming, pleases. Xarisma is where we get the word charisma. Xarisma means "Grace-gift", the ability to carry out or Divine empowerment (hence the -ma suffix) to carry out God's plans here on earth. The plural form xaristmata literally means "Grace **endowments**."

Please note I bolded disposed and endowments. These two words stood out to me, and I want to look closer at them. *Disposed* means "to give a tendency to." Endowments are "free and natural provision." Grace is a gift of free and natural provision. Jesus himself told the disciples, "If you then, being evil, know how to give good gifts to your children, how much more will your heavenly Father give the Holy Spirit to those who ask Him?" (Luke 11:13, NASB).

Grace (*xaris*) is a multifaceted word, much like God is multifaceted. Grace is the root of xarisma (grace endowments/grace gifts/"spiritual gifts") and xarismai (pardon; show favor and kindness) and has a much deeper meaning then what we may have learned in the church. I think church teaching has tried to box grace in just like it has tried to box God in and since God cannot be boxed, neither is the term *grace* in the New Covenant. Grace encompasses the New Covenant: what Jesus did at the cross for us in the complete exchange; what we walk in right now in this moment knowing that the sacrifice Jesus made at the Cross was completed; the understanding that I am a new creation; freedom, I can't do anything to earn it, I just receive it; Jesus in me; me in Jesus; who I am now in Christ; and all of His benefits. Grace is so difficult to define or fully understand that it has taken an entire New Testament to write about. We can no longer narrow it down to just the gifts of the Spirit or just to Christ wiping away sin. Yet, it is multicolored, multifaceted, and we need to bring it out of the box and actually live in it. Grace is exactly what James was talking about when he said, "Let me show you my faith by my works." This is God in us. I don't want to diminish this statement. God, the very creator of *all* things sent his son to die so he could come live in us and with us at all times. This is grace. It is big, and when I think about it, it simply astounds me at his goodness. Because of God's grace, we are able to give favor, mercy, compassion, forgiveness which are wrapped up in the term *grace*. The ability for us to do those things listed above comes because of God's grace. Grace, the root word, comes from our father in heaven through his son Jesus, which then births all the rest of the facets in and through us.

Here is what the Lord brought to my attention to illustrate or give me a picture of exactly how this looks: the term *Eucharist* means:

> gratitude, from eucharistos grateful, from eu- + charizesthai to show favor, from charis favor, grace, gratitude.

If you notice the word *grace* is in the middle of the word *Eucharist*. Eucharist is another term for the Lord's Supper when Jesus told his disciples that his body is the bread and his blood is the wine of the New Covenant (Matthew 26:26–29). We eat the bread and drink the juice/wine, which represents his body and blood. We consume him in remembrance of him (1 Corinthians 11:25). He, in bodily form, is divine grace in its fullness. He and his promises internally becoming one with us. What we do when we consume the bread and wine (juice) physically represents what he has done spiritually. We are to stand in the remembrance of *all* that Jesus has done for us and in us. It is as real as the bread and juice we take in. It is the binding contract of grace and salvation eternal that he performed all by himself on the cross for us.

This New Covenant, set up from the foundation of the world, was the contract signed by the blood of Jesus when he chose to substitute his life for ours. Jesus brought grace through his death and he brought eternal life through his resurrection—the New Covenant. Grace is what we believers not only walk in daily but also lives in us. When we understand grace, we can walk in full assurance of who we are in him. Once I grabbed hold of all he did for me, I began to trust him more and more, which allowed me to naturally walk in what James calls "faith with works." I naturally, without my "doing the work" like I had in the past, grew more like Christ. I never feel like I have to perform for him to love me. Even if I never do another "Christian act" in my life, he still will love me right where I am at. My core belief had changed to see him for who he truly is and see myself for who I am in him. I think I like the way Paul says it in Romans 5:1–11 (MSG):

> By entering through faith into what God has always wanted to do for us—set us right with him, make us fit for him— we have it all together with God because of our Master Jesus. And that's not all: We throw open our doors to God and discover at the same moment that he has already thrown open his door to us. We find ourselves standing where we always hoped

we might stand—out in the wide open spaces of God's grace and glory, standing tall and shouting our praise. There's more to come: We continue to shout our praise even when we're hemmed in with troubles, because we know how troubles can develop passionate patience in us, and how that patience in turn forges the tempered steel of virtue, keeping us alert for whatever God will do next. In alert expectancy such as this, we're never left feeling shortchanged. Quite the contrary—we can't round up enough containers to hold everything God generously pours into our lives through the Holy Spirit! Christ arrives right on time to make this happen. He didn't, and doesn't, wait for us to get ready. He presented himself for this sacrificial death when we were far too weak and rebellious to do anything to get ourselves ready. And even if we hadn't been so weak, we wouldn't have known what to do anyway. We can understand someone dying for a person worth dying for, and we can understand how someone good and noble could inspire us to selfless sacrifice. But God put his love on the line for us by offering his Son in sacrificial death while we were of no use whatever to him. Now that we are set right with God by means of this sacrificial death, the consummate blood sacrifice, there is no longer a question of being at odds with God in any way. If, when we were at our worst, we were put on friendly terms with God by the sacrificial death of his Son, now that we're at our best, just think of how our lives will expand and deepen by means of his resurrection life! Now that we have actually received this amazing friendship with God, we are no longer content to simply say it in plodding prose. We sing and shout our praises to God through Jesus, the Messiah! (Romans 5:1–11, MSG)

Works naturally come after faith just like the cart does after the horse or the egg comes from the chicken. Works are not something you perform, but how the Holy Spirit, who has come to dwell in you, performs as you abide in Jesus. If the works are the focal point then we have definitely put the cart before the horse. Our focal point needs to start with the truth of all God did through his son on the cross and in the resurrection for us, just like John the Baptist was reminded to do. This way we eat from the Tree of Life and won't stumble over who Jesus is. Even James understood we needed to put the cart before the horse because he also said this in his letter, "Every good act of giving and every perfect gift is from *above, coming down from the father* who made the heavenly lights; with him there is neither variation nor darkness caused by turning" (James 1:17).

IS THE FLESH REALLY
ALL THAT BAD?

How exactly do we, the branch, naturally change when God, the vine, comes to live inside us? Where does it work? Just our spirit? What about our body and soul? What will help us answer these questions, and many others, is a better understanding of how God intricately created our body, soul, and spirit; where he resides within us; and how much he loves the way he created us. Let's begin with the soul and spirit in Hebrews 4:12:

> For the word of God is living and active and sharper than any two-edged sword, and piercing as far as the division of soul and spirit, of both joints and mar-

row, and able to judge the thoughts and intentions of the heart. (NASB)

In this scripture, Paul talks about the word of God dividing the soul and spirit. How many times have you been taught the flesh (body) or soul is bad and causes you to sin and this is why the writer of Hebrews says it needs to be divided? When we actually look a little deeper, this is not what the writer meant at all. Believers, both Hebrews and Gentiles, back in the days of the apostles, had a very different idea about the body, soul, and spirit because they understood God's intricate design of humans. So where exactly did this teaching come from? In the past, I had been told by Christian leadership the above scripture meant I needed to ask the Lord to divide my soul and spirit because one was evil and the other was good. This belief system, in this church, came from reading Watchmen Nee's book *Latent Power of the Soul,* which the counselor, who was on staff at this church, had told the leadership to read. The leadership was trying to give an answer as to why we still sin as believers. According to the counselor and the female lead pastor, if we asked God to divide the soul and spirit, we wouldn't be double-minded, we would have more control of sin in our lives, and we would just be much happier all the way around. At the time I thought this made sense because my core beliefs did not line up with God's truth. My core belief still stated: I needed to make God happy with me, and I should be able to be performing perfectly for God all the time because for Pete's sake, I have the Holy Spirit living in me! I believed I had power in myself (with

God's help of course, but I needed to make it happen by being good) to overpower my corruptible self, if Paul could do this… I should be able to also. I asked for the counselor and female lead pastor to pray for the separation of my soul and spirit. Things did not go so well for me after we had done this. I felt…off. These are the best words I could find to describe how I felt inside myself. When I asked God about what was going on with me, he told me he never asked me to separate my soul and spirit. I then asked him to put me back together again and to repair what I had asked to be divided. After I brought this to the leadership, they also quit. At the time, I didn't fully understand why this was incorrect. It wasn't until after God started changing my core beliefs that the light bulb went on.

When I read Watchmen Nee's book, I can find some things I agree with, such as:

- spirit is God-given
- soul is God-breathed life
- body is God-formed

Like I said before, one of the prevalent beliefs I have found in Christianity, for a long while, is the belief the soul is evil and the spirit is good. This same belief is echoed in Watchmen Nee's preface in his book, *Latent Power of the Soul*:

> The spirit and the soul are two totally different organs: one belongs to God, while the other belongs to man. By what-

ever names one may call them, they are completely distinct in substance. The peril of the believer is to confuse the spirit for the soul and the soul for the spirit, and so be deceived into accepting the counterfeit of evil spirits to the unsettling of God's work. [4]

I want to counter what was stated above by Nee. Nee's belief system is prevalent within "Christian circles" and "the church building." To understand why Nee is incorrect with his statement and belief system, we need to go and look at the Greek meanings of the words *body*, *spirit*, and *soul*. This will help us understand how the early Christians understood how we were formed by God into the being we are.

First, the *body*. In both the Greek and English, the definition is pretty straightforward. It is our skin, bones, organs, and muscles.

Easy enough to explain our body, yet what becomes a little more difficult to explain is our soul and spirit. Let's look at the Greek for *spirit* next:

spirit (4151) pneuma—properly, spirit (Spirit), wind, or breath. The most frequent meaning (translation) of 4151 (pneúma) in the NT is "spirit" ("Spirit"). Only the context however determines which sense(s) is meant. This is the spirit

---

4   Watchmen Nee, *Latent Power of the Soul*, preface, pg. 3.

of man: the vital principle by which the body is animated; the power by which a human being feels, thinks, wills, decides; is the rational part of man, the power of perceiving and grasping divine and eternal things, and upon which the Spirit of God exerts its influence; (πνεῦμα, says [Martin] Luther, "is the highest and noblest part of man, which qualifies him to lay [h]bold of incomprehensible, invisible, eternal things; in short, it is the house where Faith and God's word are at home")[5]

Next the Greek and Hebrew for *soul*:

soul (5590) psuche—the soul is the seat of affections and will; psyxḗ (from psyxō, "to breathe, blow" which is the root of the English words "psyche," "psychology")—soul (psyche); a person's distinct identity(unique personhood), i.e. individual personality.[6] The Hebrew word for soul is nephesh and means: life, self, person, desire, passion, appetite, emotion.

---

5 "Strong's Concordance," biblehub, accessed 2014–2019, https://biblehub.com/strongs.htm

6 biblehub, "Strong's"

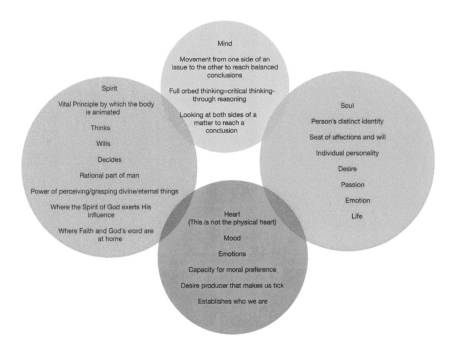

Both the soul and spirit contain similarities in what they contain (see pic). Many times I have heard it taught our mind, will, and emotions are within our soul; yet according to the Greek and Hebrew they are a part of both our soul and spirit. I would like to propose, it just isn't that simple or concrete to define the soul and spirit the old way; and Hebrews 4:12 shows us exactly why we can't. If we were to apply this same logic of dividing the soul and spirit to our bone and marrow from the scripture, this would be devastating to our body. This may have been why I didn't think this was accurate in the past. What is Hebrews 4:12 really saying?

In context, the writer of Hebrews had been speaking previously in his letter about entering God's rest, resting from their works and not hardening their hearts to the truth of what they are hearing of "true rest" from works (Hebrews 4). Hebrews 4:12 starts with the word *living*, which in the Greek means "I am alive." Then goes on to say "for the word." *Word* in Greek is *logos*, which means "word of God."

God has purposefully created humanity to have a connection with Him through faith in both our heart and mind.

According to biblehub.com, the Greek word *logos* is used 330 times in the New Testament and is preeminently used of Jesus Christ (John 1:1). I propose, because the Hebrews writer was speaking of entering God's rest, that the use of "word of God" and "life" here meant that Jesus Christ, "logos of God," is alive and active (effective, productive of due result, at work) within us. Jesus Christ, because the Hebrew writer is making it clear to Hebrews that God is Triune (God, Jesus, Holy Spirit), is also the only one who has the ability to see us clearly even to the point of being able to divide between joint and marrow or spirit and soul. This helps explain just how completely intertwined we are by God's design.

The Greek word *diiknoumenos* is usually translated as "piercing or penetrating." The rest of the definition for this word found in Hebrews 4:12 goes on to be defined as "passing through." Also, Hebrews 4:12 is the only occurrence in the New Testament this particular word is used with this definition of "passing through." This is very important for us to understand because it helps us know, God is the only one who can pass "pierce" through and see where the spirit ends and the soul begins.

The next word *division* comes from the Greek word *merismos* (3311), which is only used twice in the New Testament. *Merismos* can be further described as "division to that most hidden spot, the dividing line between soul and spirit, where the one passes into the other." As you can see, the Hebrew writer was trying to explain how God is the only one able to penetrate and see the dividing line where one passes through to another for both our bone and marrow or our soul and spirit. He is also the only one who can judge the inward thoughts and intents of our hearts.

Our soul and spirit, like with bone and marrow, are both vital and necessary parts to our structure. We can't say bone is good and marrow is evil or vice versa because each serves a specific purpose to our bodies. It is the same with our spirit and soul. Each serves their necessary purpose and they need one another. It makes up who we are as individuals. You cannot say one is more important than the other because both are needed. The soul makes up our unique personhood. It is who we are created to be. This makes up our personal identity, and God does not want us checking this at the door when we come to him through his son, Jesus Christ. He created us individually and loves what he created. God breathed his life into us making us a living being with a soul, which gives us our personality; so why would he want us to essentially cut this part out of our living being? Our uniqueness was created by our Creator, and this uniqueness is needed by the body of Christ, so it can contain all of the body parts needed by the body (1 Corinthians 12).

Another argument for loving your soul is actually found in Luke 10:25–28:

> And a lawyer stood up and put Him to the test, saying, "Teacher, what shall I do to inherit eternal life?" And He said to him, "What is written in the Law? How does it read to you?" And he answered, "YOU SHALL LOVE THE LORD YOUR GOD WITH ALL YOUR HEART, AND WITH ALL YOUR SOUL, AND WITH ALL YOUR STRENGTH, AND WITH ALL YOUR MIND; AND YOUR NEIGHBOR AS YOURSELF." And He said to him, "You have answered correctly; DO THIS AND YOU WILL LIVE." (NASB)

I used to read this and have many questions and maybe you have too. Questions like: Can I love God with all of me all of the time, I mean really 100 percent of me, and how can I love my neighbor or God when there are times I don't even love myself? *This is impossible.* I will always fail even with Christ in me. I just could not live up to these expectations. As I came to understand every good gift comes from God above, the Old Covenant (precross) and New Covenant (postcross) were never meant to mingle; and all of me, the branch, rests (abides) in Jesus, the vine, then I thought maybe what I have believed Jesus was saying to the lawyer in the past was wrong. Exactly what was Jesus telling the lawyer? The Greek gives us the answer we are looking for. First the meaning of the Greek body parts:

heart (2588)—kardias—The affective (mood, emotions) center of our being and the capacity of moral preference. "Desire producer that makes us tick" establishes who we are. This is not the actual physical heart.

soul (5590) psuche—the soul as the seat of affections and will; psyxē (from psyxō, "to breathe, blow" which is the root of the English words "psyche," "psychology")—soul (psyche); a person's distinct identity(unique personhood), i.e. individual personality. The Hebrew word for soul is nephesh and means: life, self, person, desire, passion, appetite, emotion.

strength (2479)—ischus—strength-have force to overcome immediate resistance.

mind (1271)—dianoia—from 1223 /diá, "thoroughly, from side-to-side," which intensifies 3539 /noiéō, "to use the mind," from 3563 /noús, "mind")—properly, movement from one side (of an issue) to the other to reach balanced-conclusions; full-orbed reasoning (= critical thinking), i.e. dialectical thinking that literally reaches "across to the other side" (of a matter). ("critical thinking"), literally "thorough reasoning," incorporates both sides of a matter to reach a meaningful (personal) conclusion.[7]

Next the context is interesting because when Jesus had stated what was expected of the lawyer, the lawyer still wanted to justify (make himself "right with God") himself by asking another question, "Who is my neighbor?" It is so human of him and us to desire to perform well or prove ourselves worthy for God. The lawyer believed he had done all Jesus had told him he must do in loving God and his neighbor. Yet, Jesus made it clear the lawyer had not fulfilled the entire requirement because Jesus saw into the lawyer's heart and saw something. Jesus answers the lawyer's question by teaching about the Good Samaritan who helps a man on the road. Obviously, Jesus knew the Jewish lawyer, within his heart, did not see the man on the side of the road as his neighbor because he told the lawyer to go and do the same.

I believe there is a hidden message in Luke 10:25–28, which may not have been clear until Jesus died and rose again. Within the story, there are two key words, which reveal this

---

[7] biblehub, "Strong's"

secret and will help us. The first key is when Jesus told the lawyer, "Do this and you will live." *Live* used here is the same as *life*, and Jesus is the way to life for all people (John 14:6). The second key is the Greek word *Agapeo* (love) used by Jesus and it is defined as:

> love (25) agapao—properly, to prefer, to love; for the believer, preferring to "live through Christ" (1 Jn 4:9, 10), i.e. embracing God's will (choosing His choices) and obeying them through His power. 25 (agapáō) preeminently refers to what God prefers as He "is love" (1 Jn 4:8, 16). See 26 (agapē). With the believer, 25 /agapáō ("to love") means actively doing what the Lord prefers, with Him (by His power and direction). True 25 /agapáō ("loving") is always defined by God—a "discriminating affection which involves choice and selection" (WS, 477). 1 Jn 4:8,16,17 for example convey how loving ("preferring," 25 /agapáō) is Christ living His life through the believer.[8]

From the above definition, *agapao* is our preference, our selection, our choice to have Christ come and live in our heart, soul, strength, and mind. The natural result of Christ coming to live in us through the Holy Spirit leads to our ability to *live* or have *life*. Many Christians have

---

[8] biblehub, "Strong's"

been taught that Christ comes to live in them, but only in their spirit. In the above definition of *spirit*, it references Luther's opinion that the spirit is the place "where faith and God's word are at home." Just because this is where they feel at home does not mean this is the only place the Holy Spirit dwells. He comes to infiltrate every part of our being making us a new creation (body, soul, spirit) and not just a new spirit. God also prefers and chooses (loves "agapeo") to fully intertwine himself, as his Holy Spirit, within every aspect of our whole being. This is one of the reasons why the Christ, his son, was sent to earth and why he died. Life in us, eternally. Jesus was telling the lawyer *life* comes from our choice to have him come and live within our entire being.

What I desire for each of us is to understand is who is living inside them and rest in this belief. Once again we are the branch, and he is the vine. God lives intertwined with his beloved and because of this it is easy to hear God, be changed by God, talk to God, and have a relationship with him. His desire is *always* toward you.

GOD IS REALLY BIGGER THAN ANY BOOGEYMAN

In the last chapter, I spoke of how Nee and many Christians today are so afraid of their soul. One of those reasons is because they are afraid of "soulish" prayers. This belief stems from fear and not believing God is big enough nor is he a good enough Father to us to be able to listen to our hearts and still love us. When we believe it is our responsibility to make sure we don't "pray soulish prayers," we are living from a place of pride believing we can do all things through ourselves; but when we understand prayer is just communicating with God, spirit to spirit, we can understand there is no such thing as "soulish prayers." He already knows what is going on inside every part of you and loves you. God knows our heart's true intent (good or bad), even when we don't, and he still loves us.

The other reason Nee and many Christians think we should separate our soul and spirit is to make sure demonic beings could not inhabit us. I do not believe when we, as Christians, are filled with God there is room for demonic beings within us. Can they bother us externally? Yes…but I believe the only way they can bother us is if we believe they can—this is an example of being tormented because you are believing a lie and passing it down as truth (chapter 5). The belief demons can come into a believer's soul sets up a fear, within each of us, which then becomes the very thing that opens up the ability for the enemy to mess with you. The enemy knows who he can pick at, and it all starts with what they believe in their core, not what they say they believe (professed beliefs). Faith (belief/trust) is more powerful than we realize in the western world. The western world is just now starting to catch up to the eastern world, realizing there is something to belief that we need to understand more deeply.

Other ways Christians, today, believe Satan can have access into our lives is by our bad behavior "sin" in our lives, choices to watch certain movies, reading certain books, going certain places, and talking or having any connection with certain people.

Years ago, as a stay-at-home mom of two young toddlers, my husband and I had gone back to church. In the many churches, books I read and other well-meaning Christians I would hear: God is omnipresent, omniscient, and he has Satan under his foot. Yet, I learned by the behavior I watched, some of the books I read, and soon by my own experiences, the enemy is allowed to attack you, your family, your business, and your friends; or he can come and harass you in your house. Anytime something bad would happen in our lives, the next question out of our last pastors' mouths was, "Where is the sin in your life? What did you do wrong? Where did you go? What book did you read? What movie did you see? Or, what words did you speak?" If there was nothing found that I had done, maybe it was something a family member did or how about a generational curse from a family member's actions who is now dead? The enemy sounded and felt like he had carte blanche (full discretionary power). Of course I was told, "Oh no he doesn't have full discretionary power...he has to ask God first before he does anything; then God either lets him or not." Whether or not God lets him or not was fully dependent upon me asking God to forgive me for my behavior or asking forgiveness for the deceased family member's behavior. This teaching then fits the belief: God is all powerful because God allows these "enemy attacks" because of my, my family's, or deceased family's behavior "sin." My bad behavior or the bad behavior of an ancestor (generational cursed) caused me to be cursed, and if I didn't repent immediately, for me or them, the attack would begin and wouldn't stop until I had repented for either myself or my ancestor.

Behavior, behavior, behavior. Everything in my relationship with God was tied to my behavior. This is not at all what the early Christians believed. I believe this belief began in the Holy Roman Church. The Holy Roman Church, in an effort to control people, emphasized behavior over faith when they took over Christianity. This belief has filtered through all churches from all denominations because all churches we see today have come out of the Holy Roman Church, whether we like it or not, even the nondenominational church. Humans feel a need to make themselves better, and there are those in church leadership who like to have control; all we have to do is look at history. With this root, need, and belief, the church body has passed from one generation to the next by process content learning from one another the need to look at our behavior (the leaves of the tree) and return to the tree of knowledge of good and evil. This belief has led many people within in the church to "fake it til they make it" in both leadership and the congregation. They look at their leaves and pretend they look good all the time. They try to hide those brown leaves of "bad behavior" and pretend they aren't there (1 John 5–10). The brown leaves always come forward though because God wants to help us and the only way he can is when we acknowledge them (1 John 5–10). We can see how important those leaves are to everyone within the church, by the fact that when bad stuff does come out about leaders or congregation members (like lying, cheating, pornography, stealing), people can't handle the truth and blame God or blame the leaders/people for being human and failing; instead of remembering we all fall short of the glory of God.

Growing up, we all learned by watching others live their lives whether at home, school, or church. Like I said before, when we spend a lot of time with people, we pick up their mannerisms, etc. All of us process content learn as we grow up. We have learned at home, school, and at church, if we attended, our behavior either earns us positive or negative consequences. This is a fact within the earthly world but is not a fact in God's kingdom for those who believe in Jesus choosing to live under the New Covenant. One of my favorite examples comes from the story of the workers who got paid the same wage even when they did not work the full day (Matthew 20:1–16). The workers who had worked longer were upset they were paid the same amount as those who had worked a shorter time. Now you know this would not float in our society. We go to work and fully expect to get paid for how long we work. Jesus was making it known God's kingdom is different than the earthly realm. In God's kingdom, we are all equals when we come to Christ. We are also equal as we all live in Christ.

Within the earthly world, God has created the deep magic within the foundation of the world (yes I take this from C. S. Lewis because it is such a great description[9]). This describes sowing and reaping (Galatians 6:7). This fact is process content learned quickly as we grow up and we learn: if you speed too many times, you will get caught; if you steal, you will get caught; or if you lie enough, you will get caught. Getting caught holds natural consequences here on earth such as tickets, fines, jail time, and people not trusting you to name a few. These "natural consequences" come from our choices and are a reality here on earth. There is a difference though in our horizontal human relationships (earthly) and our vertical relationship with God (kingdom). Here on earth, with our human counterparts, we will make mistakes, hopefully want to make amends, and regain trust with our family, friends, and others we

---

[9] C.S. Lewis, *The Lion, the Witch and the Wardrobe*, pg. 155.

may hurt when we make choices and decisions which have hurt them.

In my horizontal relationships, there were many times I have yelled or said things to my two boys where I went back and had to say sorry. I would do the same with my husband, my family, and my friends when I had done something to hurt them. Did I make the same mistake again? Sometimes. Did I go back and apologize? Yes. The truth is, we are human, and we will always fail to be perfect. When we understand we all fall short, it helps us to not only see ourselves as imperfect, but it also helps us to see our imperfect selves in others and have compassion.

Our vertical relationship with God is different. It is one where the divine came to make a way for us to have a relationship with him once again. Jesus is our propitiation (gained our favor back with God), he is the door, and he fully mends our relationship. This is why we cannot compare our horizontal human relationships, which bear natural consequences, to our vertical God relationship where our consequences of eternal punishment and separation from God have been cleared when we accept his free grace gift. God sees us as already forgiven because his son paid the penalty for our sins. This is challenging for us, as humans, to understand. We can't always seem to separate the two types of relationships we have because we learned as we grew up natural consequences were a part of life and the church teaches God is angry with us if we don't act right. While all the time, God is saying he made the way for us through his son. It is difficult for humanity to believe God would come down in the form of man, take on all of our punishment we deserve from our acts here on earth, fully pay for them with his life, and when we accept his free grace gift, we are automatically clean and seated in heavenly places for all time. We didn't have to do anything to deserve what we just freely received. It baffles our human mind.

The church teaches, because God is angry with us for our "bad behavior," we must apologize to him. Relating our relationship with God to man. Mixing the horizontal and vertical relationship. Because of this core belief we have many in the church teaching and believing if we repent for our "earthly sins" or "bad choices," then God will take away our earthly consequences. This just isn't true or biblically factual. I have heard stories regarding this false belief system. One of those stories was a woman who refused to pay her speeding ticket. She believed God would take care of it because she had "repented." This isn't what happened. Instead, there was a warrant put out for her arrest. What she needs to know instead is there is a helper to walk with her through the earthly consequences. This doesn't mean she won't feel peace, love, encouragement, and wisdom through it all; but it does mean she needs to take responsibility for her choices. Best of all, God isn't mad at her. He isn't making her suffer, he isn't trying to make her learn a lesson (this is already formatted into our world, the "deep magic"), and he doesn't need her to beg for forgiveness from him as he has already forgiven her. For those in Christ, all of the heavenly consequences for our poor choices (sin), which would cause separation from God, have already been taken care of by Jesus. Earthly consequences for our choices though still stand. For those found in Christ, we always have a helper to walk with us through the earthly consequences.

Not all "bad things" that happen to you are from your "poor choices." We need to see how intricately intertwined our horizontal relationships are. Our choices have ripple effects on others and their choices have ripple effects on us. What exactly did the early Christians (pre-Holy Roman Church) believe about "bad things" happening to them? When we look at their lives, we begin to realize in this life there will be trouble/tribulation (John 16:33); and this trouble does not always occur because we were "bad," it is simply a part of this life. It is a part of this life because we live in a fallen world, which contains fallen people making choices, which impact all of our lives. Jesus himself let us know…there will be trouble in this world; yet, he gives us peace (wholeness), and we are to look through this tribulation to the fact he has overcome this world. Jesus's overcoming this world does not equate to our only having all roses as long as our behavior is good, as many believe now; but *in him*, no matter what our behavior or what is happening to us, we can have real peace. Life challenges are going to happen, even when your behavior is good, and he is *with us* through the tribulation, even when your own behavior and choices were not "good." All of this was made very clear to me the day I visited the Roman Colosseum in Italy.

When I was in Rome walking the roads many early Christians had and stood in the shadow of the Colosseum, I had a sensation of standing in a place in the time period I live in, yet also standing back in the time of the early

Christians. I could close my eyes, and it was like I was transported back in time. I could feel, smell, and see back to the times of Paul. I knew Paul may have walked in the same streets I was walking on. I knew so many early Christians had definitely walked on these same streets. As I stood in this moment with my eyes closed, peace fell on me; and I heard and understood:

We all have our storms we must weather.

A recent story and a story from my past came to my mind. The story from my past was when I was in high school, and although I had done nothing that would even hint toward what would be whispered about me, it didn't stop the rumor that I was pregnant from going around the school. I went home devastated, and my mother told me that the truth would come out. Which of course was an easy one since in nine months there was no pregnancy or baby. I think for most of us our name being dragged in the mud or lies/rumors being told is painful. Rumors can ruin people's lives and livelihoods. When my name, once again, began to be dragged through the mud a few years ago I wanted, just like I wanted in high school, to find out where it started from and confront the person or persons. I was rightfully angry and felt wronged. I think it is difficult for anyone to sit back and listen to what is being said about you that is not true.

Right after returning from our trip, one morning, I suddenly woke up feeling so much peace. I hadn't asked for it, I hadn't prayed for hours, I hadn't done anything.

Only because God loves me and he resides within me does he know what I need whether spoken or unspoken. Over the next few days, the peace continued and one morning I distinctly heard the Lord say to me:

> "It is time to let go of the need to
> clear your name. Trust me."

When He stated this, I knew this is exactly what he had done for me...taken away my need to clear my name and gave me peace. I felt safe. This came from the inner-most place within me, my heart.

Please remember: I didn't do this for myself or go through any particular steps, God simply did it for me, in his time and exactly when I needed it. And he will do the same for you because he loves you and desires the best for you (Luke 11:13).

To help me understand what he had done, he used the story of Jesus in the boat from a book I had read two years ago: *30 A.D.* by Ted Dekker. In this book, I had high-lighted some things:

1. "And why does man get angry? Because he feels threatened or wronged. And why does he feel threatened? Because he does not feel safe."
2. "No threat in a rumor."
3. "Nothing in this world threatens you."
4. "Release the fear your understanding shows you in the storm... By trusting Me instead, not the storm and not the boat."[10]

---

[10] Ted Dekkar, *30 A.D.*, pgs. 333, 318, 335, and 352 (in order, digital copy).

Like the disciples I had been walking in little faith (trust, belief) because I was fearing the storm and my safety just as they had in the boat. Now, with a better view of God, I saw the story so much clearer than before: Jesus was not mad at them for waking him, and he wasn't mad at me for lacking faith. He was letting them know what they really needed from him and growing their faith in him. He was helping them see him, in their boat, with them was the greatest thing in the world. No storm could change the fact Jesus was in their boat with them, which means he is in my boat, in me, and no storm can change this. What I was beginning to understand is nothing in this world threatens us, as believers (faith in, trust in) in Christ, because we have inherited eternal life through Christ. This doesn't mean there is an absence of fear, concern, or worry. What it does mean is no matter what, Christ is with us now and forever...no matter what. This is how I knew Christians could walk into the Colosseum and face such horrible things. They lived from the belief Christ is with them always, no matter their circumstances, only because they first believed. Nothing else mattered.

Early Christians understood God had a greater plan, and he meant good for them even when it didn't look good. They knew this life on earth was fleeting and saw God's end plan of eternity with God. Once again, this never meant they didn't have fear, concern, worry, or any of the human emotions we have when facing horrible things at the hands of other people's choices, sickness, or death. Our peace gift from God means we are whole, no longer broken; we have eternal life; and God is always with us. Jesus overcame this world by his one act of obedience on the cross which gives us the right to live eternally with God. This overcoming gave us access to the Tree of Life. Because of this core belief, I believe, they were able to face horrible things and still hold on to Christ. Our generation needs this understanding too. We have given Satan a place in our lives which does not line up with the New Covenant. We have said he has all this power, when he doesn't. People make terrible choices that impact other people. We live in this fallen world, with both the weeds and wheat and sometimes bad things happen to us. Yet, out of these bad choices people make, God does bring good; we may never see it or it may not be the way we want it to look, but it does happen. This doesn't mean there won't be heartache, pain, loss, sickness, death, or problems. But he walks with us in these times, always. These bad things aren't allowed because you didn't do something for God. We do have earthly consequences to our behavior and choices, but God is not angry with us and is not asking for these bad things to happen to you.

Letting go of my boat (my name being cleared) didn't make what was done to me right, just like what was done to the early Christians was right or good. It also doesn't mean I won't speak truthfully about what happened to me or what happened to the early Christians. For me letting go of my boat meant I no longer needed my "end result" to feel safe, peace, or happy because: I knew God has a larger plan. Your boat—whatever that may be: your good name, your finances, your abilities, your good health, etc.—is not what we can put our trust in because they will always fail. The storms which come at our boats we look through to the fact, Jesus has given us his best by giving us access to the Tree of Life (eternal life with him).

Storms happen because we live here on earth, and God is walking with us through them all the time. But what if we do choose to watch a "wrong movie," read a "wrong book," go to the "wrong place," or heaven forbid, a "spiritually dirty person" or heathen touches you? These were real fears and concerns within the last church my family attended. You were taught, by their behavior, you must keep yourself holy. Don't taste, don't touch, and don't go was their motto. This core belief led to a very fearful life for both me and my children. I had taught my children, as they watched me, to live in fear of wrong people, movies, books, video games, music, places. This led to a picture of God, which was distorted for us. This false belief system has been taught in many churches, which has caused many churches to close themselves off from people or ideas that may actually help them.

I ended up on the receiving line of this very belief in our last church because I was labeled as Jezebel, rebellious, and Satan himself by the leadership. This label gave people the reason to make me the enemy. This belief and labeling led people to believe their hatred and believing they were holier led to very hurtful acts not only toward me and my husband, but also toward my children who people actually believed they were "infected" by me. My children lost all friendships they had within this church almost overnight. It was sick. How can good Christians treat people so poorly? *Fear.* Fear is a strong emotion. The leadership used fear as their tactic to keep people away from us by saying

I am "filled with demons" and, if they come close to me or my family, have a relationship with us or are even our Facebook friends these demons will jump on them, create more demonic warfare for them, demons will attack their children, and they will fall away from God. This is a perfect example of when people believe Satan is bigger than God.

Even when I still had a distorted view of God, I had helped many people afflicted by the demonic. At times, I believe it probably would have been better if I hadn't read books or listened to others teach me how to help people get free from the demonic because Holy Spirit was always there to help me. I didn't fear helping people get free from demonic influence, but there were many times I was called to help in situations or would simply be at the right place at the right time to help someone and because of my own false core beliefs about God, I would question if God was big enough *in me* this day. Was my behavior good enough, my slate clean enough, or my faith strong enough to deal with this person who was dealing with the demonic? I was constantly in fear of going anywhere wrong, watching anything wrong, reading the wrong book, or touching someone who could give me a "hitchhiker." This fear is what allowed the enemy to have a place to bug me or harass me. So what changed for me and what needs to change for Christians like me?

It is all about what we believe in our core. As my core beliefs aligned more with the truth of who God is and what he has done for me, which shows me who I am in him, this caused me to be able to see exactly where Satan is now. Living from the correct core beliefs, will cause us to actually walk in sync with our professed beliefs. I am the daughter of the Most High God, and I know this within my core because of Christ. This knowledge causes me to walk in the confidence the enemy has lost, he has no right in me or around me, anything he tries to whisper and accuse me of I profess—I am the righteousness of God in Christ Jesus (Romans 3:22, 1 Corinthians 1:30, 2 Corinthians 5:21, Philippians 1:11 and 3:9, Galatians 2:21). I know I never stand in my own goodness or badness—I only stand in what Christ has done. I know who I am and whose I am to the very core of me. In wisdom, anywhere I go with him I am covered, protected, and loved. I can touch everyone, have relationship, and talk to anyone, and I will leave the mark of Christ's love because he lives in and through me. I change the very atmosphere of anywhere I step my foot.

One of my favorite stories is when I met an old friend at a funky coffee shop between where I live and where she lives south of me. This place advertised they might have ghosts. In the past, I wouldn't have dared go there because I truly believed (which brought the torment), like the Disney ride, a ghost would hitchhike back home with me. Now armed with what Christ has done for me (the truth of who I am in him), instead of getting a hitchhiker at this coffee shop, I was aware of the fact I brought his light in there. Nothing touched me, I was not harassed, we didn't get sick… I, my family, nor my friend had any problems at all. Actually my friend experienced a huge miracle in the days that followed our get together. Isn't this just like God? I want freedom for those still bound in fear. I want freedom for all those that are afraid to be near me or others who are looked at as "evil" or "spiritually dirty." This false belief system causes Christians to fear going places, seeing people, touching people (who probably need a touch), and has brought divisiveness within friendships and families. There is no reason anyone who considers themselves to be Christian should be afraid to talk to people both inside and outside the church. If your core belief really is "God is bigger and he is love," then you walk this out in your daily life. This is exactly what one of my friends said to the female lead pastor who told my friend to "let go" of our friendship because of "my demons." My friend responded, "If this is true, when I leave work today, I am going over to her house and that demon is going to be gone!" Right there is the core belief God is bigger being walked out in her life. She knew exactly who she is in Christ and whose she is. Your actions tell the world what you really believe. What are your actions saying about your beliefs?

Jesus didn't promise us a nondirty, easy life but one where we would be sent out like sheep in the midst of wolves; but he is *always* with us.

> "Behold, I am sending you out like sheep in the midst of wolves; be wary and wise as serpents, and be innocent (harmless, guileless, and without falsity) as doves. [Gen. 3:1.]" (Matthew 10:16, AMP).

How are we wise as serpents with still being gentle and knowing who we are in Christ? Wisdom is given by God to everyone (Proverbs 2:6). We are either wise or foolish when we choose to listen to wisdom or not. Let me give some examples. You are a woman like me, and you think it is okay to walk down a dark alley by yourself at night... ummm, wisdom says maybe not smart, so you decide to go a different route. Use wisdom not fear when going places, reading things, watching movies, etc. But please know this, reading a particular book, watching a certain movie, going to a certain coffee shop, or touching a person will never be able to make you lose your salvation. Another example using wisdom is when a young woman had a friend asking her about tarot cards, and she decided to seek out wisdom from an older woman, me, asking me what I think about this subject. I explained to her, I believe tarot card readers are opening the door to the spiritual realm without Jesus, which means they are accessing the spiritual realm illegally. So, you will get a mixed bag when you seek knowledge, understanding, or future events this way. The mixed bag means you will get some truth mixed in with some lies and a sprinkle of fear. Jesus on the other hand opens the door legally to the spiritual realm, and he always gives you truth. I explained to her I am no longer afraid of the tarot cards or the people using them. I can touch and be around both without the fear of being "demonically attacked" or getting a "hitchhiker" because God is bigger than all that, and he lives in me. I asked her, "Do we need to seek a tarot card reader to get our answers?" And I answered the question with wisdom, "Why seek something inferior when you already have the answers you need inside you?"

Why seek something inferior when you already have the answers you need inside you?

Just like with the tarot cards, we do not need to fear reading something, watching something, or playing a certain video game. We do need wisdom when choosing. Is this something worthwhile? Is it something for me personally? Does it help or hinder? These are all good questions. My oldest son, when he was little, had night terrors. We finally watched *Monsters Inc.* this year...yes, he was nineteen. Wisdom. Wisdom will help you parent and make choices. Everyone is given wisdom.

Jesus told us to walk in wisdom, yet be gentle. As you can see, both of these qualities do not involve fear but love and compassion. Compassion is created when we can see our own flawed selves in others while wisdom, through the Holy Spirit, gives us the best way to love someone and make choices.

COULD I REALLY LOSE MY SALVATION?

In the last chapter, I talked about how I used to believe going to certain movies, reading certain books, having certain items in my house would invite a demon "hitchhiker" into my house to harass or harm my family, friends, or me. I see many Christians taking it even further by believing they can lose their salvation by any actions deemed "bad enough" to them. I believe when someone holds to the belief, "Any of our 'bad' actions could cause us to lose our salvation," it stems from the idea some sins are bigger than others.

Before going further, I need to admit a couple of things. First, I really didn't ever believe I could lose my salvation. Yet, I was part of a church where the leadership did believe this in their core. I had always wondered why they were so afraid of certain things, which were shown by their behavior and choices. I finally had proof this was what they believed when one of them slipped and admitted it to me once. Second, I had heard about the unforgivable sin, but I didn't understand what it really meant to blaspheme the Holy Spirit. I did see and understand Christians were afraid of both of these things because it meant they would no longer live with God but go to hell. I want to take an in-depth look at both of these incorrect core beliefs and show through scripture we, as Christians, do not need to live in this fear anymore.

Let's first start with the belief we could lose our salvation. Many Christians believe in levels of sin, and there are those sins, which are "bad enough" to cause you to lose your salvation. I, thankfully, started with the viewpoint every sin is a sin in God's eyes because when I first met my husband, Bryan, he was the one to explain this to me and I believed him. It made sense, even though I had been raised Catholic. In my understanding, Catholicism believes some sins had to be atoned for more than others; thus the requirement to say ten Hail Mary's instead of only four this time. I believed for many years that a sin is a sin in God's eyes until years later I had told this to the female colead pastor from our last church. She corrected me, told me there is a "greater sin," and I needed to go look it up. I did and as I read the verse in John 19:11, with my core beliefs not lining up with the truth of what God has done for us, I thought, "Oh no! I have thought wrong for my entire Christian life…there is a greater sin." I immediately felt fear and became even more insecure in my relationship with God. I realized later this is exactly where some Christians form the idea they can lose their salvation if they do something "bad enough" on the scale of sin behavior. The idea where some sins are bigger is a viewpoint held by human thinking formed out of the Old Covenant. I know you immediately went to Leviticus and started thinking of the different atoning requirements written for different laws broken such as an eye for an eye, death by stoning for committing adultery. We have learned that we don't want to mix the Old Covenant into the New anymore. In the New Covenant, the kingdom of heaven sees Jesus atoning for all of our actions for all time. We also know this is so we will always and forever have a relationship with God, Jesus, and the Holy Spirit. Keep in mind, there are consequences in the earthly realm regarding our choices; but from the kingdom perspective, we are fully forgiven and pure as the driven snow in the New Covenant. What exactly is Jesus saying to Pilate when he uses the words *greatest sin*?

When we enter this part of the story, we find Jesus standing before Pontius Pilate the second time, after he has already been scourged. Pilate has stated he finds no fault in him and the Jews answer back:

> We have a law, and by that law He ought to die because He made Himself out to be the Son of God. Therefore when Pilate heard this statement, he was even more afraid; and he entered into the Praetorium again and said to Jesus, "Where are You from?" But Jesus gave him

no answer. So Pilate said to Him, "You do not speak to me? Do You not know that I have authority to release You, and I have authority to crucify You?" Jesus answered, **"You would have no authority over Me, unless it had been given you from above; for this reason he who delivered Me to you has the greater sin."** As a result of this Pilate made efforts to release Him, but the Jews cried out saying, "If you release this Man, you are no friend of Caesar; everyone who makes himself out to be a king opposes Caesar." (John 19:7–12, NASB)

When read on the surface, it appears there is a "greater sin." When your core beliefs have shifted to see God for who he is, then you know there has to be more to the story. The English translation of the word *meizona* (3173) above lacks the depth of the full Greek meaning. Meizona (greater) is an adjective describing the noun *hamartian* (266). Let's first look at the meaning of the Greek word *hamartia* (266) again:

> sin (noun)= hamartia 266 = (ha) not and (3313 meros) a part or share of; no share ("no part of") loss **(forfeiture) because not hitting the mark. Every action or decision done apart from faith.**

And now the adjective describing the noun hamartia:

(3173) megas: (meizona) large, great,
in the widest sense. Things to be esteemed
highly for their importance, equivalent to
Latin "gravis" (heavy, serious, important);
specifically of great moment, important.

This is when God gave me a picture for further understanding: I saw Pilate standing feeling quite in power with
the ability to choose life or death for a person and laud-
ing this over the head of Jesus. Pilate believed he held all
the power in this moment, but Jesus made it very clear in
his full statement to him he really did not have any power
except what was given to him by Jesus's Father in heaven.
Jesus then went on to let Pilate know he didn't have the
most important, weightier action, or decision done "apart
from faith." Judas's betrayal, and the High Priest's handing
Jesus over to the Roman authorities were of much more
significance to this moment. The English word *because* in
John 19:11 is "dia (1223)" and it is the root of the English
word *diameter*, literally meaning "successfully to the other
side."

God had purposefully given authority over Jesus (this
would be the only time this occurred), which allowed the
rest to take place successfully. There was one who had
made the weightier or more important "self-empowered"
choice of delivering Jesus to them, which brought them
all to this place at the other side of the diameter or circle
(see diagram). The High Priest and the rest of the religious
elites had chosen, of their own free self-will, to deliver Jesus
to the Roman government to be tried and crucified. The

Roman Empire represents the Gentiles who still were also ruled by self-empowerment (sin). We need to remember at this time all people, Jews and Gentiles, were all subjects (self-empowerment "sin" ruled mankind) to self-empowerment "sin" because Christ had not yet died and rose again. Self-empowerment (sin) ruled through men on earth still. The only reason self-empowerment "sin" had any ability to do anything to Christ at this time is because God had given power over his Son to man.

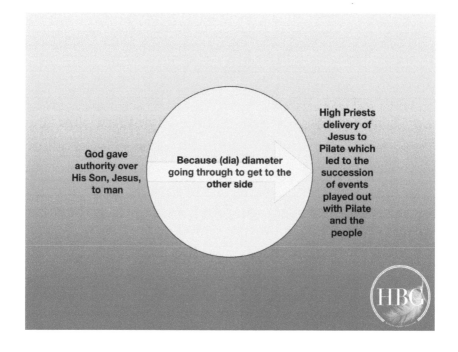

God gave authority over His Son, Jesus, to man

Because (dia) diameter going through to get to the other side

High Priests delivery of Jesus to Pilate which led to the succession of events played out with Pilate and the people

Jesus was letting Pilate know four things: (1) The ones who had delivered him to Pilate had made the more important, weightier self-empowered "sin" choice to get him to this point; (2) Pilate wasn't as important as he thought himself to be, he only played a small part in history; (3) In this moment, the realization hit Pilate that he was not as in control of this historical moment as he perceived himself to be; and (4) Pilate, himself, needed to know who Jesus really was. God always goes to the furthest star to reach each and every one of us, exactly how we need to be reached. Right after Jesus's statement, Pilate decides it is not such a good idea to crucify Jesus and leaves it up to the people to decide. This is stated in John 19:12–13, 15–16:

> As a result of this Pilate made efforts to release Him, but the Jews cried out saying, "If you release this Man, you are no friend of Caesar; everyone who makes himself out to be a king opposes Caesar." Therefore when Pilate heard these words, he brought Jesus out, and sat down on the judgment seat at a place called The Pavement, but in Hebrew, Gabbatha.
>
> So they cried out, "Away with Him, away with Him, crucify Him!" Pilate said to them, "Shall I crucify your King?" The chief priests answered, "We have no king but Caesar." So he then handed Him over to them to be crucified. (NASB)

I honestly don't know whether Pilate believed in who Jesus was in this very short exchange between him and the son of God. Pilate though did have an inscription written on the cross in Latin, Hebrew, and Greek which read:

"JESUS THE NAZARENE, THE KING OF THE JEWS." Therefore many of the Jews read this inscription, for the place where Jesus was crucified was near the city; and it was written in Hebrew, Latin and in Greek. (John 19:19–20, NASB)

Just like with Pilate, Jesus comes to each of us in our own individual way and lets us see him and know who he is. Each of us is on our own individual journey and on that journey we will all have the opportunity to choose to believe in the son of God or not. As humans, we don't need to look at our own journey and judge it according to where you have been, are at now, or even how you might look in the future. What God wants us to do is look at the grace gift of righteousness he gave through his son as he lives in us through his Holy Spirit. The truth is, Jesus makes us righteous in the New Covenant our actions or lack of actions do not make us righteous. When we are able to believe, within our core, we are only righteous through Jesus we will be more capable to love ourselves, others and see ourselves for who we are in Christ; we aren't afraid of our lack or bad mistakes and are then able to live more freely from the inside out by having the ability to be open and honest because we know God loves us anyway; and we are more free to be ourselves and talk about what is going on, on the inside of us, with trustworthy people, without the fear of being judged by God or others.

Much of what we see today as a lack of real love in the church body, I believe stems from incorrect core beliefs regarding God and ourselves. When we base our holiness on our actions instead of Christ's actions, then we desire to look at someone else's behavior and say, "Look, they are performing much worse than I am," to help ourselves feel better about ourselves. Jesus said we would be known for our love for one another. Yet, when we are comparing ourselves to others, looking for the greater sin, it is difficult to love ourselves much less love others. The enemy enjoys when Christians believe there are levels to sin because we end up working so hard for something we already have received for free. Jesus came to level the playing field for all people. No greater sin, no greater people. We are all equally in need of Christ; his payment is equal for each of us just as he said with the workers in the vineyard, and we are all equally holy in Him.

Jesus came to level the playing field for all people.

When I live from the core belief, we are all equal in Christ, and God loves us equally no matter what we have or haven't done. It gives me the ability to be honest with myself and others regarding my limitations, mistakes, and inability to be a "perfect Christian." This is where we truly let go of the reins, the driver's seat; however, you want to see it and let God take over. Honesty should not lead to condemnation but freedom, knowing God loves us and accepts us all the time right where we are at. When we try to fix ourselves, we sit in the driver's seat instead of God, who is the only one who can take us from glory to glory. In the past, I believed I had to perform things like holding my tongue, not lying, think on what is pleasant, pray for hours, please God in every thought and action in order to stay in favor with God. Yet, God is saying: "I take you from glory to glory. You don't. This is my job." Once I let go, I let myself off the hook. So much of my time and energy had been put into making God happy to keep the boogeyman away and proving I "was saved" I was exhausted. I found myself exiting a prison cell I had already been set free from with Jesus's act, but I had kept myself in with my own core beliefs. I repented and understood once again, God sees all "sin" equally. His son has taken care of all "sin" on the cross by proclaiming, "It is finished." No sin is too big, too consistent, or too bad for Jesus's blood.

If Jesus's blood is strong enough for any wrongdoing done, then what about the "unforgivable sin" known as blaspheming the Holy Spirit? The second way many Christians believe they can "lose their salvation" comes out of the scripture in Mark 3:28–30. I personally know this statement has caused much fear with many Christians. I had prayed for a handful of people who had so much fear because, usually as a young person, they had been told by an adult leader in a church they had committed the unforgivable sin (blasphemed the Holy Spirit) and would not be able to go to heaven, *ever*, no matter what. Both of my boys, in their Christian studies classes, experienced this same teaching. They were trying to be convinced there was an "unpardonable sin" they could do, which would bar them from heaven forever. Thankfully, each of these occurrences had happened after my three-day revelation and both boys knew better. My youngest child got in such a heated discussion with his "Christian studies teacher" that he had to be pulled out of the classroom. For him he saw a God that would forgive everything and the way this teacher was explaining this scripture to him, in Mark, did not fit into his view of God. I am hoping to bring clarity, hope, freedom, and truth to this scripture that has because of the way it has been taught for many years, either put people in fear believing they have lost or could lose their salvation forever.

I want to look at two different translations of this verse. One from the New King James Version (NKJV) and one from the Message (MSG). My favorite is from the Message, yet many times this verse is taught within the church from the NKJV translation:

> "Assuredly, I say to you, all sins will be forgiven the sons of men, and whatever blasphemies they may utter; but he who blasphemes against the Holy Spirit never has forgiveness, but is subject to eternal condemnation"—because they said, "He has an unclean spirit." (Mark 3:28–30, NKJV)

"Listen to this carefully. I'm warning you. There's nothing done or said that can't be forgiven. But if you persist in your slanders against God's Holy Spirit, you are repudiating the very One who forgives, sawing off the branch on which you're sitting, severing by your own perversity all connection with the One who forgives. He gave this warning because they were accusing him of being in league with Evil" (Mark 3:28–30, MSG).

What I find even more interesting is the title in the NKJV for this section is titled, *"The Unpardonable Sin."* This right there was enough to scare me and lead me to wonder, "Have I ever done the unpardonable sin without even knowing it?" Let's get the bigger picture by starting with the context. At this point in Mark's story, Jesus was healing and teaching around Galilee. There were many people from other areas there with him. He had just chosen his twelve disciples, when all of a sudden scribes are proclaiming Jesus to have the prince of demons, Beelzebub, within him. Jesus turns to them and asks them several questions, "How can Satan cast out Satan? If a kingdom is divided against itself, that kingdom cannot stand. If a house is divided against itself, that house will not be able to stand. If Satan has risen up against himself and is divided, he cannot stand, but he is finished! But no one can enter the strong man's house and plunder his property unless he first binds the strong man, and then he will plunder his house" (Mark 3:23–27, NASB).

Right after this, Jesus then goes on to say in Mark 3:28 how *all* of the sins and blasphemes will be forgiven the sons of men. It isn't just a few sins but *all*, which means in Greek the totality of. All "results of self-empowerment" or "calling what God disapproves as 'right' will be forgiven." It will be fully accomplished and finished for all time. Then, all of a sudden, it sounds like Jesus is now retracting what He just said in the next two sentences. But He isn't. I looked up each word in the Greek in all three verses. Specifically verses 29 and 30. Here is what I found:

> Whoever refuses to acknowledge the good that has come from the union (remember Jesus is talking about Himself and the healing He has been performing by casting out unclean spirits) of the Holy Spirit, negates possession of forgiveness in this age, is legally bound or obligated eternally (both now and outside of time) to "the results of self empowerment" because they have concluded I possess a spirit which is adulterated("a wrong mix'/ tainted by sin). (Mark 3:29–30)[11]

He is making it clear there is one condition that the son of man (this is you and me) must choose to make to have *all* your sins forgiven. But the scribes had just concluded that the *sinless lamb was full of sin*. For them, unless they change their minds (which means repentance) and realize that Jesus is the sinless one who will take on all of the son of men's sins, they are negating the *only* way to possess forgiveness from God. Jesus truly is the only way to God.

Jesus was already telling how and who forgiveness would happen through. How the one condition of faith in who he is makes all the difference for the sons and daughters of Adam and Eve. It is the same simple message of

---

[11] http://biblehub.com/text/mark/3-29.htm and http://biblehub.com/text/mark/3-30.htm)

faith, forgiveness, and a spotless lamb who must be seen as spotless not just as a "good man," a "prophet," or a fake.

When we choose to see Jesus as the spotless lamb, for who he is, all countercovenants are replaced with the New Covenant where all transgressions and iniquity are cleared and death no longer reigns through self-empowerment. Many, from the past, wished they would see this happen when living under the Old Covenant (Luke 10:24 and 1 Peter 1:10). These scribes continued to want to see themselves, their traditions, and their sacrifices as the only way to God. They wanted to remain under the Moses covenant. The scribes had no interest in changing their core beliefs at this time. Jesus was there ready and willing to help them change their core beliefs to God's way of seeing things (true repentance), but instead they chose to hold on to their old beliefs. Maybe like me, this made them feel safe and what Jesus was saying and doing scared them or maybe they loved their power and wanted to keep control over the people. Either way at this time they were not ready to change their way of belief. They were not ready to repent and see Jesus for who he is for them. Many today are in the same boat as the scribes. They do not want to admit Jesus is the sinless lamb who came to make the way to God. Like the scribes, their faith and trust are in other things. This is the one and only thing, which cannot be forgiven. Jesus will never force himself on people; it is always a free will choice. This means there is no way you can "lose your salvation." Like all of a sudden, you believe in him then you lost it because of something you have done, said, read, watched, or touched. It is only your belief or unbelief in Jesus, which gives you access or denies your access to eternal life with God. Even when someone is choosing unbelief or does not yet know who Jesus is, God continues to pursue them just like he did with the one lost lamb (Matthew 8:12–13).

MISSING THE MARK

Remember I asked the question in chapter 3: How could Jesus say, "Go and sin no more"? In chapter 3, I began to understand faith, unconditional love, who I am in Christ, freedom from condemnation, freedom in Christ, how *he* took all her sins, how he wiped her slate clean, how he fulfilled the law, and his approval of her. Simply stated, I was beginning to see who I am in him and all he had done for me. But years later, I still questioned how could Jesus tell her to go and sin no more, how could Paul say to the Romans we are dead to sin? Why do I still "sin" if Jesus said, sin no more? He finally answered my question four years later...

Within chapter 5, we learned the definition of *sin*, which is the Greek word *hamartano* (264). Let's revisit this word and also two more words tied to it:

1. 264 hamartano (VERB) from 1 /A **"not"** and **3313 /méros, "a part, share")—properly, having no share in**; to sin, **which always brings forfeiture—i.e. eternal loss due to missing God's mark**. Like 266 /hamartía, 264 (hamartánō) is regularly used in ancient times of an archer missing the target (Homer, Aesch., etc). **Every decision (action) done apart from faith** (4102 /pístis) is sin (Ro 14:23; cf. Heb 11:6). See 266 (hamartia).

2. 265 hamártēma (a neuter NOUN derived from 264 /hamartánō, "to sin")—a sin, **focusing on its result** (note the -ma suffix), i.e. "the painful linkages of sin." See 266 (hamartia). [265 (hamártēma) **emphasizes the consequences of making any decision (action) by self rather than of faith** ("God's inworked persuasion," cf. Ro 14:23).]

3. 266 hamartia (NOUN) ("sin, forfeiture because missing the mark") is the brand of sin that emphasizes its **self-originated (self-empowered) nature**—i.e. it is not originated or empowered by God (i.e. **not of faith**, His inworked persuasion, cf. Ro 14:23[12]

First, I want to point out each of the Greek words above talk about

- faith,
- missing the mark,
- self-empowerment, and

---

[12] biblehub, "Strong's"

- consequences to self-empowerment, which bring about forfeiture and eternal loss.

Further down in the definition of *hamartano* it states:

> To be without a share in, namely the mark; to miss the mark with the genitive (which expresses the possession, source, origin) of the thing missed; then to err, be mistaken; lastly to miss or wander from the path of uprightness and honor, to do or go wrong.[13]

The definition above is important because it gives us the ability to better understand what the scriptures within the New Testament, which has been translated from Greek to English, are actually saying to us. This is not going to  involve any interpretation on my part. Only the definitions that prove there is more to this than meets the eye.

In answering my question, the Lord did several things for me. He started with a statement and gave me a picture to help me understand. Lastly, he proved what he said to

---

[13] biblehub, "Strong's"

me through scripture. As I was finishing my first edit of this book, the Lord distinctly said to me,

"I told the woman to go and miss me no more. Hold on to what happened here and not let go or give up her belief in me, for anyone or anything."

Keeping her faith in Jesus was *all* that was expected of her. At the same time, he said the above statement to me, I again saw a bull's-eye (see pic at left) where Jesus was the mark to hit. He is always perfection, the bull's-eye. No other human being can ever fulfill all or hit the bull's-eye (perfection in every thought or action). Mankind either chooses to believe in him and reside within him (within the bull's-eye) or remain on the outer circle (outside him). I want to make it clear there are not some Christians who are closer to Jesus because they behave better than others. We are either believers, who because of Jesus abide in him in the bull's-eye, or unbelievers, those still on the single outer ring outside the bull's-eye, no levels here either. We are in or out...that simple. We all (all humanity) started on the outside of the bull's-eye (mark) because everyone falls short of the glory of God. Only faith in Jesus puts you within Jesus (the bull's-eye). I was shocked by this new revelation to say the least because this is not what I had been taught both verbally or by process content learning within the church. This isn't what anyone has learned that I know of. This explanation finally put everything together for me and finally pronounced, "It is finished!" It also answered exactly how and why Jesus could tell the adulterous woman to go sin no more. I now knew I really could go and "sin no more."

The woman caught in adultery is not the only person Jesus tells to "go and sin no more." He also says this to the man he healed at the Pool of Bethesda. Jesus didn't say this to the man when he healed him, but later after the man had been caught carrying his mat on the Sabbath and had been questioned by the Jews. It was against the law to do any work on the Sabbath and the man caught carrying his mat, was working. The man, when questioned, informed the Jews there was a man who healed him who told him to pick up his mat and walk. Now the Jews were mad at the person who healed the man too. Who could be "sinning" by healing (working) on the Sabbath? After this confrontation, Jesus finds (yes, Jesus was literally searching for him) the man in the temple. Jesus tells him, "Behold, you have become well: do not sin anymore, so that nothing worse happens to you" (John 5:14). Sounds ominous, doesn't it? At the surface this seems like Jesus is telling him, hey you better clean up your act and make better choices in your behavior or else you are going to get sicker or have some terrible fate awaiting you. I believe many of us have learned, in the church, if we sin one more time maybe God won't forgive us; we will get sick, a family member will get sick, we will have something happen to us or our loved ones like a car accident. We have read John 5:14 this way because our core beliefs come from a place of fear and not love. We see God as a mean God and not one who reaches out to us no matter our circumstances, even if we have done something wrong because this is what we have learned for years in the church. Have you ever heard or maybe said: God is gonna get you, God is gonna spank me, God is mad at me, or you better straighten up and act right and be obedient or else? All of this comes from a wrong core belief.

The root of our belief system has been fueled by the understanding God is mad at you because (1) our translation from Greek to English is lacking in the fullness of what is being said, and (2) we have mixed the Old Covenant into the New. This has caused scriptures, which contain the words *hamartano*, *harmetia*, and *hamartema* when translated as *sin*, in the English Bible, to be completely misunderstood. We have been taught when we see the word *sin* in English we are to automatically think bad behavior, a wrongdoing, a slipup, or falling away from God; but there are other Greek words whose definition do contain these words. The problem with this way of translating does not give us a full picture of what is actually being said so that we can understand what the author of the letter intended.

To help us get the fuller picture, we need to start from scriptures, which reference hamartano, then move to supporting scripture. When we finally realize the fullness of God's plan, you will never be able to say you are not good enough for him, yourself, or others ever again. You will live completely free in him. Not worrying if you have done enough for him, been obedient enough, been good enough…you will finally find the resting place Jesus promised. Don't you want to?

Let's begin with Hebrews 11:6 (contains the word *faith* = *pistis*) and Romans 14:23 (contains *faith* = *pistis* and *hamartia = self-empowerment*), which are referenced scriptures within biblehub's Strong's concordance of all the above Greek words for *sin*. First Hebrews 11:6, which had been translated into an active voice in chapter 9:

> God has pleasure when we believe, trust in, cling to, rely on Him.

Second is Romans 14:23:

> But he who doubts is condemned if he eats, because his eating is not from faith; and whatever is not from faith is sin. (NASB)

Like us today, the Roman Hebrews had a difficult time not mixing the Old and New Covenant together. They had questions like: should we circumcise or not, and should we eat food sacrificed to idols or not? What mattered and what didn't? Please tell us what to do Paul? Sound familiar? Paul is helping them, not by directly answering their question, but by helping them know what is important. Let's add some further definition to the words used in the above scripture:

> The one however vacillating (over-judging, doubting), if he eats is condemned (establishing guilt), because [it is] not [an] outcome (out of the depths of this source and extending to its impact on the object) of faith/belief/trust; everything now (as the logical result of what precedes; in light of

what has gone on before) that [is] not faith/ belief/trust, is self empowerment not God empowerment (266 hamartia). (Emphasis and further definition added is mine from Strong's Concordance at biblehub)

Simply stated: "However the one doubting, if he eats establishes guilt, because it is not an outcome of faith; everything in light of what has gone on before (Jesus on the Cross) that is not faith, is self-empowerment not God-empowerment" (Romans 14:23; emphasis and further definition added is mine from Strong's Concordance at biblehub).

When people "believe" their own behavior causes them to be "good" or "good with God," this is "self-empowerment (266 "hamartia")." Following the law to prove one's worth is a form of "self-empowerment." In the Old Covenant, people were expected to follow the law in their own power and ability. Today, we hear in the church we should be able to do *everything* right and well because God lives in us, but what we will see soon this is not at all what Jesus or God expects from us. Again this thinking in the church mixes the Old and New Covenant together and God never intended this because they are like oil and water, which do not mix. God instead wants us to know we are "good with him" because of our faith (belief) in what God did for us through Jesus. This is *true* or *real* God empowerment; God in us.

Paul describes this in more detail earlier in his letter in Romans 5–6:4. Here again we find both (266 hamartia) and (264 hamartano) translated into English as *sin*; this again brings a lot of confusion to what Paul wrote. Within this part of Paul's letter, we also encounter a few other words, which will give us a better understanding of exactly what Paul is saying. The words of interest are transgression, trespass, condemnation, justification, death, died, life, in, and through. If you want, you can pull out a copy of the Bible and open it to Romans 5–6, just in case you want to reference where I am at. Let's first start with the definitions of the above words in order:

1. Transgression (3847) parabasis = a deviation, transgression, a deliberate overstepping of the line, willful disregard for God's law which defies His drawn lines.
2. Trespass (3900) = fall away after once being close beside; a lapse, slip, false step; a wrongdoing that can be (relatively) unconscious, "nondeliberate." The NASB does not differ in its translation of the two words above both are translated as "transgression" in the text. Causing further misunderstanding I believe.
3. Condemnation (2631) katakrima = punishment following condemnation, penalty; the exact sentence of condemnation handed down after due process (establishing guilt). As you can see, condemnation has a richer meaning in which it includes the punishment handed down after establishing guilt. As a note here when Jesus does not condemn the woman caught in adultery, it is the verb of the noun above with the exact same mean-

ing. There would be no due process, no sentence, and no punishment for what she had done.

4. Justification (1345) dikaioma = a judicially approved act with righteousness with its results.

5. Death (2288) thanatos = separation from the life (salvation) of God forever by dying without first experiencing his gift of salvation.

6. Died (599) apothnesko = away from which intensifies to die. The separation which always comes with divine closure.

7. Life (2222) zoe = it always (only) comes from and is sustained by God's self-existent life. The Lord intimately shares his gift of life with people, creating each in his image, which give all the capacity to know his eternal life. I believe this is the "seed" in each of us which is planted by God because we are created in his image we bear his seed, which through faith is activated (chapter 9).

8. In (1722) en = something which operates from the inside (within).

9. Through (1223) dia = to go all the way through successfully across to the other side. (Same word from chapter 13 with Pilate.)

Using the definitions above, I want to break down the text of Romans 5:12–6:4. In this part of his letter, Paul was making it very clear what had happened from Adam to Moses, why the law had to come in, and what God completed for us through His Son.

Adam refused to listen to God properly by choosing to act on his own empowerment which caused death, self empowerment, loss of God's portion and punishment to spread to all mankind. Abraham, before the law, was righteous because he believed (had faith) in God and this was accounted to him as righteousness. When all of the Israelites stood before Mount Sinai asking for the law saying, "Tell us what to do, so we can do it," this is self-empowerment. When Moses struck the rock, under the law, too many times he acted in his own self-empowerment and could not enter the promised land. The law had to come close beside to cause an increase in falling away after being close beside God, which causes an increase in self-empowerment. With the increase of self-empowerment, God increased his free gift of extension of himself to humanity through his son, Jesus. One righteous act by Jesus causes a *process of absolution* for all mankind to choose to receive. A pathway to righteousness, eternal life, full approval of God, and a life lived close beside God. The increase of self-empowerment gives us the ability to see Jesus's coming in the pattern of Adam. When we simply choose to believe in who Jesus is this is the process of absolution. The absolution comes through Christ for us. Absolution means a formal release of punishment, guilt, or obligation. Because we have been submerged into Christ and the punishment he received (the baptism is an act in our world of what happens to us in the spiritual world), we now walk in eternal life and the punishment of death has no hold on us. This give us the ability to eat from the tree of life and be close beside

God for eternity. (For a complete breakdown of Romans 5:12–6:4, see Appendix 1.)

I hope this is helping you as much as it helped me. One last scripture I want to look at is from 1 John 3:4:

> Everyone who practices sin also practices lawlessness; and sin is lawlessness. (NASB)

Again within this scripture "hamartia" (266) is used, which we now know means "self-empowerment." With this new understanding the scripture below opens up, and we can see what John was actually saying. John used the word (458) *anomia* in the Greek, which is translated as "lawlessness." *Anomia* is defined as iniquity, lawlessness, unrighteous, acts wickedly, and disregards proper authority. Let's add the definitions of both lawlessness and sin into the above statement:

> Everyone committing "self empowerment" also commits "iniquity, unrighteousness and disregards authority"; and "self empowerment" expresses (is) "iniquity, unrighteousness and disregards authority." (Emphasis and further definition added is mine from Strong's Concordance at biblehub)

This is pretty straightforward now. Those who have missed the mark are choosing to be self-empowered rather than God-empowered. With the choice not to believe in who Jesus is, their natural outflow will continue to be behavior to disregard authority, unrighteous (Jesus makes people righteous), and act wickedly. John is describing the part of humanity who have not yet chosen to believe Jesus is the son of God and is their superior. Their belief system is in themselves, not in God. They are the ones living outside of the mark, seen in the picture from earlier in the chapter.

Living outside the mark means you are choosing to continue to stay in the forfeiture of God's portion. In the Old Covenant David wrote, "God is our portion" (Psalm 73:26). In the New Covenant, Peter says something interesting to Simon. In Acts 8, Simon wants to purchase the power of God from the apostles, when he saw the Holy Spirit being received by people the apostles prayed for. Peter said to Simon, "You have *no part or portion* in this matter, for your *heart is not right before God*" (Acts 8:21, NASB). Peter is letting Simon know God is not his portion because he doesn't believe in who Jesus is in his heart (faith). Simon wanted the Holy Spirit by purchasing (self-empowerment) it rather than believing or having faith in Jesus. There are four other scriptures, which use the same Greek word to define "part, portion or share." What is interesting is three out of the five contrasts belief and unbelief (Acts 8:21 [above], 2 Corinthians 6:15, Colossians 1:12). The fourth time, it is used to explain territory (a plot of land) in the natural (earth) realm (Acts 16:12). Lastly, the fifth time, Jesus is talking to Martha when she complains her sister Mary is not helping her with food preparations. Jesus states to Martha, "Martha, Martha, you are worried and bothered about so many things; *but only one thing is necessary*, for Mary has chosen the *good part*, which shall not be taken away from her" (Luke 10:41–42, NASB). Mary had chosen the good part. What exactly did Jesus mean here? *Agathos* (18 good) is defined as intrinsically, in a natural way, permanently good *whether it be seen to be good or not*. This is a definition of Jesus!

Faith/trust/belief in Jesus is Mary choosing the good part.

Martha on the other hand is worried and bothered about "so many things." Martha, in this moment, was seeing Jesus through the law, just like the Pharisees and Sadducees did. Martha thought she would be judged by Jesus by her actions or nonactions under the law. It was expected for women to serve and take care of guests under the law. Martha was busy trying to prove her worth under the law all the while Mary choose to simply rest in Jesus. The law (our behavior) causes us to be concerned and worried about so many things. Faith in Jesus was the *only thing necessary*. Mary had chosen this, and it would not be taken away from her. Mary's faith in Jesus gave her so much more than the law ever could. Choosing the good part, who is Jesus, brings about divine closure from all of what humanity has received through Adam's one act of self-empowerment and replaces it with God freely extending himself to humanity not based on merit or entitlement, God empowerment, eternal life, a verdict of approval (righteousness), and absolution (being fully pardoned) by God through faith. Can it get any better than this?!

Throughout the accounts of Jesus's life, we consistently hear him say, "Your faith has healed you." Jesus's proclamation was not based on merit or entitlement. A person's healing did not happen because they all of a sudden followed the law to the letter or cleaned up their act. No, each time it was simple faith (trust, belief) which bestowed the bounty gift, blind of merit, or entitlement, upon each person. The person had not had to listen to God perfectly and make sure their every thought and action fulfilled the law. They simply had to believe Jesus is who he said he is.

All of this supporting information led me to better understand what Jesus was telling the adulterous woman and the man who carried his mat. The woman was brought to Jesus while he was in the temple. The Pharisees and teachers of the law brought her and said, "Teacher, this woman was caught in the act of adultery. In the Law Moses commanded us to stone such women. Now what do you say?" The text explains this was a question to trap Jesus and this is when Jesus bends down to write on the ground with his finger while the teachers of the law and Pharisees continue to question him. Jesus then straightens up and says, "Anyone without "blame, faultless and unerring" be the first one to throw a stone at her." Again he stooped down to write on the ground. When they heard this their conscience (which everyone has and is created by God) was convinced with solid compelling evidence they were not "blameless, faultless or unerring." Each of them began to go away one by one from the eldest to the last and Jesus was left alone with the woman. Jesus stood and saw no one but asked the woman, "Woman, where are they who accuse you? No one has judged you worthy of punishment?" She answered, "No one, sir." Jesus then said to her, "Neither do I condemn you (judge you worthy of punishment) go and in light of what has happened here no longer miss the mark causing you to forfeit your portion anymore."

Jesus, the son of God, first directed the teachers of the law and the Pharisees to throw the first stone only if they are blameless. No human can say they are blameless or unerring (perfect), so they had to leave. Only Jesus holds this ability. He is the only one who is blameless, perfect, and unerring and can represent the bull's-eye in the middle (God's perfection in every thought and deed). What happens next is so powerful, and it helps us better understand our relationship with Jesus even when we have done something wrong, just as this woman had. First, let's note what the woman didn't do, she didn't:

1. ask for forgiveness
2. grovel to be forgiven
3. speak out loud, "I believe in you, Jesus"
4. promise to no longer do what she did
5. she didn't even speak her thankfulness

What did she do?

1. She answered his question.
2. She received his proclamation of no judgement.
3. She obviously believed in her heart who he is because of "what had happened here."

Let's look at what Jesus didn't do:

1. Tell her she needed to be sorry.
2. Demand her to promise not to behave in a "unlawful manner" anymore.
3. Quote scripture to her—in order to prove she wasn't doing something right.
4. Kill her by stoning her.
5. Throw her away.
6. Tell her she is naughty and bad and better straighten up.

What did Jesus do?

1. He did not condemn her. He did *not* judge her as guilty.
2. He told her in light of what happened here to go and not let go of her God portion she had found in him, her superior.

Let me restate this again—Even though she had committed adultery, Jesus Christ, the son of God, did *not* judge her as guilty or in need of punishment for what she had done. All of us have done or will do something, whether in thought or deed, which deserves God's punishment; yet as we have faith in who he is, we, just like this woman, will *never* be judged as guilty before God.

I just want to remind us, from chapter 12, we still have consequences in this earthly realm for our choices. But from God's point of view we are found *not* guilty and will receive no punishment from him, just like the adulterous woman. Jesus then told her it was only logical now because of what she experienced, she should go and not miss the mark anymore. Her faith should remain in Jesus, the only one, who can pronounce you *not guilty*. He finished this work on the cross with his one act of righteousness, fully listening and being obedient to God. We rest in his sacrifice, his obedience, his righteousness, only by faith.

Jesus did the same for the man. He healed him by making him whole and then warned him to go sin no more, so something worse does not happen to him. Jesus was also letting this man know not to turn back to trusting or having faith in the law and his own behavior, i.e., do not carry the mat on the Sabbath or do not heal on the Sabbath. Our performance will never get us to the mark, *ever*. Jesus is the bull's-eye we can never perform, but because of his performance we get to live there with him in faith. When Jesus told the man something worse would happen to him if he chose to go back to the old belief system Jesus was letting him know there is only one thing, which is unforgivable and that is missing the mark, not seeing him as the sinless lamb, which is the unforgivable sin from the last chapter.

This is only thing Jesus cannot cover and that is our choice to have faith in ourselves instead of him. When we choose to not believe (faith) in him, we sit outside the mark. When we have faith in him we sit inside the mark with him, resting. We don't have to perform to be there, we rest there. We don't even have to perform our faith. We either believe Jesus is who he says he is or we don't. It is simple and easy. Just as the branch rests on the grapevine. Resting there the branch naturally bears fruit. It doesn't work hard to produce the fruit, *ever*. It naturally happens. Some branches produce more than others, and yet, we all get paid the same; we are all just as close to Jesus. We all have the same exact Holy Spirit dwelling within us in equal measure; there are no favorites because it is not based on merit or entitlement, and you are loved exactly where you are at all the time. None of this is earned by us. None of it. In this you find the easy and light burden Jesus promised, and you also find the promise, whom the son sets free is free indeed.

You can read more at my blog hisbelovedgrace4ever.com.

All numbers associated with Greek and Hebrew words are from the *Strong's Concordance Index.*

Definitions of Greek and Hebrew words found at biblehub.com.

NASB Bible version used unless noted differently.

APPENDIX 1

Scripture Reference	Bullet Points	Full-Length Version
5:12	-Self empowerment, which forfeits God's portion entered the world AND -Through the self-empowerment separation from God's eternal life entered. -In the same manner separation from God's eternal life spread to all who forfeited God's portion/acted outside of faith = self-empowerment.	Through one man self-empowerment, which forfeits God's portion entered the world, and through the self-empowerment the separation from God's life; also in the same manner to all mankind the separation from God's eternal life spread upon all who acted apart from faith.

Scripture Reference	Bullet Points	Full-Length Version
5:13	-Self-empowerment was not charged to one's account until the law existed in the world.	Until the law existed in the world; self-empowerment however was not charged to one's account when the law did not exist.
5:14	-But separation from God's eternal life ruled from Adam until Moses even on those who *did not* act apart from faith in the same way as Adam's willful disregard/ deliberate overstep of God's boundaries. -Adam is a type/pattern of the one coming.	Nevertheless, the separation from God's eternal life ruled from Adam to Moses, even upon those who did not act apart from faith in the same manner of the willful disregard/ deliberate overstep of Adam, who is a type of the coming [one].

Scripture Reference	Bullet Points	Full-Length Version
5:15	-Adam's falling away after being close beside God is *not* like the freely given God empowerment. -One falling away (Adam) after being close beside = separation from God's eternal life. -How much more instead is God freely extending himself to people and the free gift, not based on merit or entitlement, within God's extending himself—Who is Jesus Christ—will penetrate the many!	But in this way the falling away after being close beside God is not like the freely given God empowerment. If by one falling away after being close beside, the many are separated from God's eternal life, how much more did God freely extend himself to humanity and the freely given (not based on merit or entitlement) within God extending himself to humanity, which is the one man Jesus Christ, exceedingly penetrate to the many.

Scripture Reference	Bullet Points	Full-Length Version
5:16	-Even *more* the bounty gift is not like what Adam caused when acting apart from faith. -Adam's establishing guilt put into motion the punishment. *Though:* -Empowerment of God comes out of the many falling away after being close beside as a result of a *righteous act* (Jesus).	Moreover, the bounty gift is not like that which came through the one who acted apart from faith. Indeed establishing guilt of the one put into motion the punishment; however the empowerment of God comes out of "the many falling away after being close beside" as a result of a righteous act.

Scripture Reference	Bullet Points	Full-Length Version
5:17	-*If* by one act of falling away after being close beside causes separation from God's eternal life to *rule* through the one (Adam). - *Then* how much better for those who *lay hold of*: (1) the abundance of God extending himself to them *and* (2) freely given, not based on merit or entitlement, gift of divine righteousness (approved of God). -*All* of this along with God's eternal life rules through the one, Jesus Christ.	If the one falling away after being close beside causes separation from God's eternal life to rule through the one, how much better for those who lay hold of the abundance of God extending himself and the freely given gift (not based on merit or entitlement) of divine righteousness, within God's eternal life rules through the one, Jesus Christ!

Scripture Reference	Bullet Points	Full-Length Version
5:18	Under these circumstances: -Through one falling away after being close beside punishment penetrated into all mankind. *so also* -Through one act of righteousness penetrates to all mankind and puts into motion a process of absolution (pardon) for God to be able to share his eternal life.	Under these circumstances, just as through one falling away after being close beside, to all mankind penetrated punishment, so also in this same way through one act of righteousness penetrated to all mankind put into motion a process of absolution (a pardon) for God to share his eternal life.

Scripture Reference	Bullet Points	Full-Length Version
5:19	Exactly as: -Through the one who refused to listen properly, which had sprung from an opposing attitude, many were made losers of God's portion. -Through the one who submitted to what is heard (Lord's voice) many will be made righteous (just in God's eyes).	For just exactly as through the refusal to listen properly (springing from an opposing attitude of God) of the one man, the many were made losers of God's portion by missing the mark, so also through the submission to what is heard (Lord's voice) of the one, the many will be made righteous (just in God's eyes).

Scripture Reference	Bullet Points	Full-Length Version
5:20–21	*Next:* -Law naturally comes in close beside, *which causes* -Abundant falling away after being close beside to God *However:* -Where self-empowerment abounded in number—God freely extending himself to humanity abounded beyond that. *So that's just exactly as:* -Self-empowerment ruled within separation from God's eternal life. -God's free extension to humanity rules through the verdict of approval of God— *This results in:* -God sharing his eternal life through Jesus Christ, the absolute owner (Lord) of us.	Next the law naturally came in close beside, so that the falling away after being close beside to God abounded in number; however where the self-empowerment abounded in number, God freely extending himself to humanity abounded beyond so that just exactly as self-empowerment ruled within the separation from God's eternal life, so also the free extension of God to humanity rules through the verdict of the approval of God, resulting in God sharing his eternal life, through Jesus Christ the absolute owner of us.

Scripture Reference	Bullet Points	Full-Length Version
6:1	-What shall we say then? -Should we continue on in self-empowerment so God will freely extend himself more?	Therefore what shall we say? Should we continue on in self-empowerment in order to have God freely extend himself even more?

Scripture Reference	Bullet Points	Full-Length Version
6:2	-Never may it be! -Why can it never be? -Anyone who separates (stressing divine closure) naturally away from the self-empowerment so how (where it is thought strange when one thing has established itself and another has not been abolished) could we experience God's life in it? *Side note: To Paul and those he is speaking to, they understand when one thing is abolished and another has been put in its place there is no way you can do both because one is no longer there.*	Never may it be! Anyone who has divine closure naturally separates from self-empowerment, so how could we still live in it?

Scripture Reference	Bullet Points	Full-Length Version
6:3	*Or:* -Are you ignorant that the many who are submerged unto Christ (are in union with Christ) = being submerged within his punishment (we are no longer punished because we are living from within Christ's punishment for us)	Or are you ignorant of as many that are submerged (baptized) into Christ Jesus, into the punishment of him are submerged (baptized)?

Scripture Reference	Bullet Points	Full-Length Version
6:4	-We are buried with Christ, through the submersion, into the punishment he received. This means he received our punishment and we never will as we are in Christ. -Because of Christ (his punishment, death, and waking up from what lacks life) we receive: "a waking from what lacks life, living from the place of God's eternal life. -This has brought us full circle.	Therefore we are buried along with him through the submersion (baptism) into the punishment of Christ, so that just exactly as Christ woke up from out of what lacks life through the intrinsic worth (glory) of the Father, so also we in newness of God's eternal life walk.

ABOUT THE AUTHOR

Darlene Gaston has been blogging on hisbelovedgrace4ever.com for the past four years with over 165 posts and counting. Her blog has reached hundreds of people throughout the United States and the world. She is a wife to her husband, Bryan Gaston, for twenty-two years and a mother of two grown boys, Taylor and Cameron.

CPSIA information can be obtained
at www.ICGtesting.com
Printed in the USA
LVHW052348100720
660358LV00008B/399